South E Dornier

South Bank, Cleveland,
15 January, 1942

Bill Norman

Bill Norman
2008

Published in 2008 by
Bill Norman, 23a Thames Avenue,
Guisborough, Cleveland, TS14 8AE

ISBN 978-0-9547325-2-3

Other books by the author

Wartime Teesside
Luftwaffe over the North
Failed to Return
No. 640(Halifax)Squadron, Leconfield
Broken Eagles (Luftwaffe Losses over Yorkshire, 1939-1945)
Luftwaffe Losses over Northumberland & Durham (Broken Eagles 2)
Wartime Teesside revisited
Halifax Squadron (the wartime bombing operations of No.640 Squadron, Leconfield)

The unit crest of KG2
(*Holzhammer*)

Contents

Acknowledgements

Introduction

1. 'Missing' for fifty-five years.   8

2. Respect for a former enemy.   34

3. A bizarre ending to tragic tales?   38

4. The man who laid the first wreath: Heinz Möllenbrok.   40

5. Broken Eagles: Luftwaffe losses in Cleveland, 1939-1943.   47

6. Luftwaffe war graves in Acklam Road cemetery, Thornaby.   53

Appendix   57
(i) Luftwaffe losses in the Yorkshire area, 1939-1945

Bibliography

Acknowledgements

I would like to acknowledge the help freely given by the following when this monograph was little more than idea. I am sorry to say that several have died since that help was given but, nevertheless, I list their names to show my appreciation. John Cavanagh, Seaham; Peter Cornwell, Cambridge; Mick Coverdale, Hartlepool; Jim Cox, Dormanstown; Mrs V. Edon, Middlesbrough; Werner Feige, Germany; Richard Flohr-Swann, Germany; Manfred Griehl, Germany; Stan Haggarth, Thornaby; Steve Hall, Brighton; John Hassan, Guisborough; Peter Kirk; Derby; Gotthard Liebich, St Albans; Otto Linsner, Germany; Kurt Matern, Germany; Stuart McMillan, Skelton; Heinz Möllenbrok, ex-KG2, Germany; Walter Myers, Sedgefield; Willi Schludecker, ex-KG2, Germany; Len Smith, Bromley; Trevor Smith, Kelloe; Alan White, Houghton-le-Spring; Eva Yarrow, Billingham; Bill Young, Middlesbrough;

Thanks are also due to the Editor, *Evening Gazette*, Middlesbrough, for permission to quote from David Lorimer's article (14 October 1998), and to the Editor of *The Northern Echo* for permission to use a number of the newspaper's wartime photographs.

German Air Force terms
used in the text: Luftwaffe organization.

Staffel:
The Luftwaffe *Staffel* consisted of nine aircraft and was roughly equivalent to an RAF squadron. *Staffeln* (the plural) were numbered from 1 to 9.

Gruppe:
Three *Staffeln* made a *Gruppe*, the basic flying unit of the Luftwaffe. *Gruppen* (the plural) were numbered in Roman numerals from I to III. The full complement of a *Gruppe*, including the *Stab* flight (see below), was thirty aircraft.

Stab:
Each *Gruppe* had a *Stab* (Headquarters) flight of three aircraft.

Geschwader:
Three *Gruppen* made a *Geschwader*, which had its own *Stab* flight of four aircraft. Thus a *Geschwader* at full strength had ninety-four aircraft and was roughly equivalent to an RAF Wing. The role of a *Geschwader* was indicated by a prefix. In the case of bombers, the prefix was *KG* (combat [or bomber] wing)

Unit notation: In view of the foregoing, the notation *III./KG2*, for example, refers to the third *Gruppe* of *Kampfgeschwader 2*. The more specific *8.III/KG2* refers to the eighth *Staffel*, third *Gruppe*, *KG2*. Because *Staffeln* 7-9 made up *Gruppe III*, the notation *8.III/KG2* was usually abbreviated to *8./KG2*.

Introduction

On 27 November 1997, a group of building workers clearing land for redevelopment at South Bank, Cleveland, unearthed the remains of a Second World War Dornier Do217 bomber of the German Luftwaffe unit *Kampfgeschwader 2* (KG2). The aircraft had crashed there in January 1942, minutes after being hit by gunfire from a merchant ship anchored off Hartlepool and seconds after colliding with the cable of a barrage balloon flying high over the river Tees. The blazing bomber plummeted on to the railway sidings of a local steelworks, where it made a crater some twelve feet deep. At that time, the sidings were being used for essential war work and so, after the charred bodies of three of the four-man crew had been recovered, most of the wreckage was bulldozed into the crater and the track was re-laid. The body of the fourth member of the crew was not found.

Following the discovery in 1997, a full excavation of the site was undertaken by a team of Royal Engineers working with specialists from an RAF Bomb Disposal Squadron. They found no ordnance other than small arms ammunition – but they did recover the mortal remains of Oberfeldwebel Heinrich Richter, the missing member of the Dornier's crew. Following an extended coroner's inquest, Richter's mortal remains were buried alongside those of his comrades at the Acklam Road cemetery, Thornaby-on-Tees, on 14 October 1998

I had investigated this particular incident in 1990, while researching material for my book *Luftwaffe over the North* (1993), and I had come to the conclusion then that there was a very good chance that the body of a fourth man was still in the wreckage. Thus the 'rediscovery' of the Dornier with its tragic secret was not a surprise to me but the extent of public interest in the case did take me back a little. It most certainly made a deep impression upon an ex-Luftwaffe pilot friend of mine who had travelled from Germany to act as the KG2 Association representative at Richter's funeral.

The media interest, both locally and nationally, was comprehensive but it was the more personal manifestations of public interest that made the biggest impression: the funeral service in a South Bank church filled almost to capacity by local people, a number of whom had witnessed the crash in 1942; and the interment witnessed by some two hundred persons in a Thornaby graveyard. The striking thing for me was that all of those people participated spontaneously, without pressure. One can only speculate why they should have felt the need or the desire to attend the funeral of a former enemy, a complete stranger from a foreign land. No doubt the nature of the discovery, as well as the association of the wreckage with more dramatic times, had some effect - but one hopes that common humanity also played its part.

Among those present, no doubt, were the merely curious but there were also others who felt a closer affinity. It did not escape the notice of my German friend that there were many ex-Service personnel paying their respects on the day: men and women who had done what they perceived to be *their* duty some sixty years earlier, who had themselves 'looked over the edge' but who – unlike Richter – had lived to tell the tale. The poignancy of the moment was not lost on them. Afterwards, an acquaintance of mine who had flown Beaufighters with the RAF in North Africa described the occasion as having been *'spiritually uplifting'*, while a friend who had flown Halifax bombers over Germany claimed that the burial of Richter had been *'a most emotional experience'*. Strange comments, perhaps, when one considers that they were used in the context of a person totally unknown to all of those who were present – unless, of course, the circumstances of Richter's death reminded them of days long gone and, perhaps, of friends once known.

During Richter's funeral service, Hans Mondorf, the German Consul-General to Great Britain, paid tribute to the people of Teesside when said that he had been quite moved and surprised by the sympathy that the case had attracted in the area. He attributed that response to, what he described as, *'the sense of fair play that the British soul enshrines'*. During my researches, which span some thirty years, I have found a number of examples to illustrate that the *'sense of fair play'* to which Mondorf referred was not merely a post-war phenomenon cultivated by the passing of time. It seems that humanity towards an enemy in need also had its place in wartime, when one might have reasonably expected feelings towards a foreign foe to be running high.

At least seventy-two German aircraft crashed in Yorkshire or off its coastline during the 1939-1945 conflict (see pages 57-59) and 282 German aircrew became casualties of war: twenty-five per cent of those were captured; the rest were either killed or listed as 'missing in action'. Many of them fell to the guns of RAF fighters

The men who fought each other in the skies over England some sixty years ago faced death and destruction on an almost daily basis. They were all brave men, irrespective of their nationality. In the post-war years, the humanity to which Hans Mondorf referred and which manifested itself on occasions in more dangerous days has developed further and a number of one-time adversaries have extended the hand of friendship towards each other. I am pleased to say that, on occasion, I have been instrumental in bringing some of them together. Details of those 'reunions' can be found in my book *Broken Eagles: Luftwaffe Losses over Yorkshire, 1939-1945* (Pen & Sword Books, 2001)

Bill Norman
Guisborough, 2008

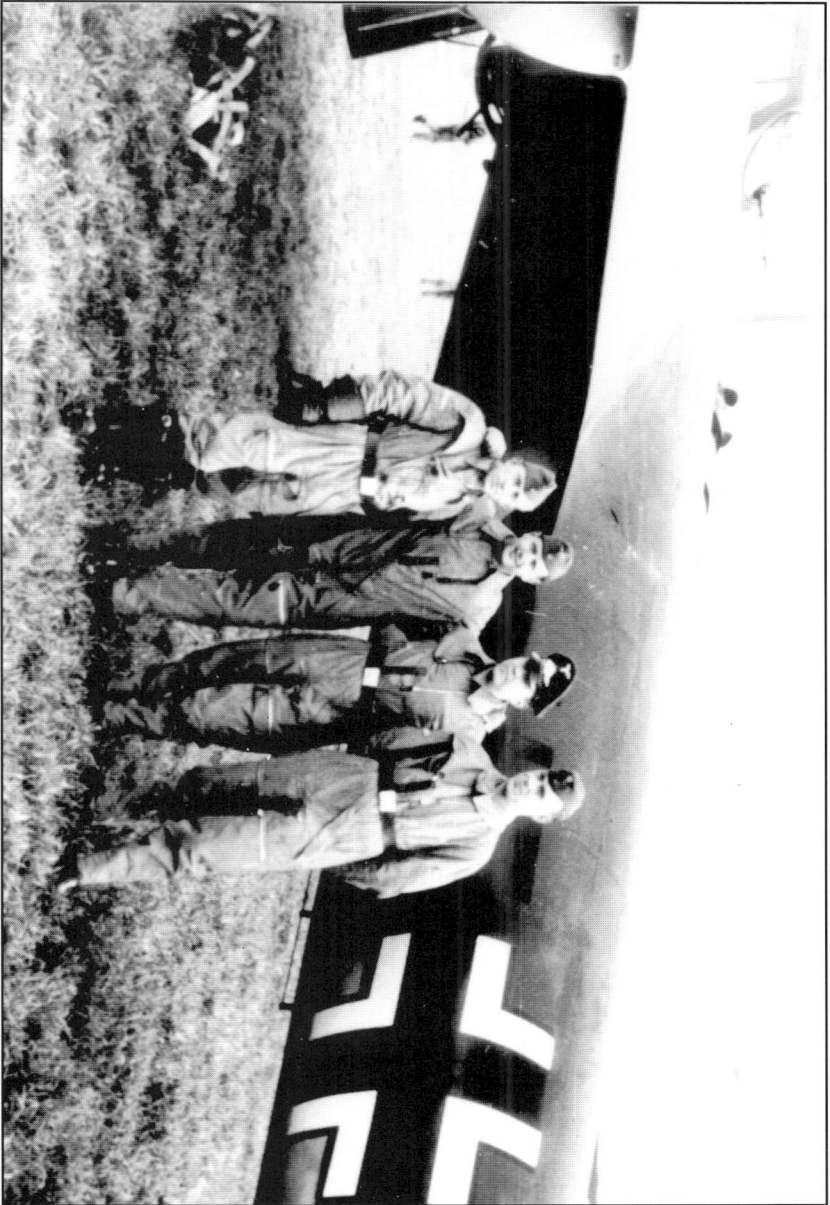

Some of the members of the crew of Do.217 U5+HS of 8./KG2: **L-R:** *Joachim Lehnis (pilot), Hans Maneke (radio-operator/gunner) Leutnant Rudolf Matern (observer/bomb-aimer), unknown. The assertion by Matern's brother that the crew member on the right is Heinrich Richter is disputed by members of Richter's family.* [Kurt Matern]

'Missing' for fifty-five years.

A World War Two German Dornier 217E-4 bomber that had crashed fifty-five years earlier was 'rediscovered' at South Bank, Cleveland, on 27 November 1997. The first pieces of wreckage were found just below the surface of the ground by Northumbrian Water Board workers laying sewers for a business park development. Following the discovery, full excavation of the site was undertaken by a team of Royal Engineers working with specialists from RAF Wittering. The aircraft, which was subsequently identified by makers' plates as U5+HS (wnr.5314) belonged to *8./Kampfgeschwader 2 (8./KG2)* and was based at Schiphol(Amsterdam). It crashed in the early evening of 15 January 1942 after being damaged by anti-aircraft fire from a merchant ship before colliding with a barrage balloon named 'Annie'.

Barrage balloons were an integral part of Britain's air defences during the Second World War and Teesside had its fair share. Forty-eight of the hydrogen-filled gas bags - 62 feet long and 25 feet in diameter - were dotted around the Tees area in an apparently random pattern and were usually flown operationally at altitudes of 4,000—5,000 feet. The prime purpose of these 'flying elephants' was not to bring down raiders: their principal function was to keep enemy aircraft at altitudes which made accurate bombing difficult while also keeping raiders at heights which allowed better targets for anti-aircraft

The crash site in 1998, after the excavation had been completed. The bomber landed in the area marked by the darker patch of rough ground. The line of the locally known Black Path can be seen just in front of the base of the fence [Author]

defences and home-based fighter aircraft. However, there were times when aircraft *did* stray into a balloon cordon: sometimes they were lucky and survived; sometimes the opposite was the case.

Any aircraft straying into a balloon cordon, particularly in darkness, was in a potentially very dangerous situation because collision with the cable that held a balloon in position would invariably stop the aircraft in its tracks and send it crashing to earth. Of course, the Germans were aware of this and thus it was most unusual for any low-flying raiders to approach barrage balloon areas in darkness. Whenever bombers attacked Teesside, which was usually at night, they generally flew at heights exceeding 5,000 feet. However, the occurrence on 15 January, 1942, was to prove a costly exception to the rule.

On 15 January 1942, Dornier 217 bombers of KG2 together with four Junkers 88 bombers of *Kampfgruppe 506* (KGr.506) based at Leeuwarden (Holland), were detailed to launch a late afternoon attack against shipping along England's eastern seaboard. An estimated twelve enemy aircraft were in the vicinity of the Tees balloon cordon between 5.34pm and 6.58pm and among them was Dornier 217E-4 (U5+HS) of the eighth *Staffel* of KG2 (8./ KG2), crewed by Feldwebel Joachim Lehnis (pilot), Leutnant Rudolf Matern (observer/bombardier), Unteroffizier Hans Maneke (radio-operator/gunner), and Oberfeldwebel Heinrich Richter (mechanic/gunner). Lehnis had been ordered to attack a convoy that was believed to be passing eastwards of Middlesbrough but it is thought that this aircraft might also have dropped one bomb on Teesside's Eston Jetty at about 5.55pm before dive-bombing the coaster *Empire Bay* (2824 GRT), one of least three vessels anchored off the port of Hartlepool that afternoon.

The reason why *Empire Bay* was in such an exposed location was due to the fact that Hartlepool was a tidal port and sea-going traffic could use it only when the tide allowed. Furthermore, such traffic could sail in and out only during daylight hours: night-time use was prohibited because lights were forbidden by the blackout regulations. Therefore, the steamer had left port when the tide and regulations allowed and was waiting to join a south-bound convoy that was sailing down the coast from the north. Thus in the late afternoon of 15 January 1942 *Empire Bay* was in a potentially dangerous situation for any merchant vessel in wartime: it was sitting at anchor and in approaching dusk, without the protection a convoy might offer and prey to any marauding enemy

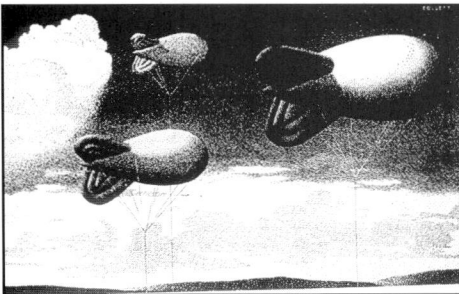

bomber - but there was little option.

Some days later, at a subsequent Court of Inquiry, Captain E.S. Parks, master of the *Empire Bay* explained that the vessel had been bound for London with 3,800 tons of coal.

'We left Hartlepool at 1700 hours and at 1715 we anchored in Tees Bay to await the convoy. The number of crew, including myself, two Army and three Naval gunners, was twenty-eight. We were armed with a 4"-gun, two Hotchkiss, four Strip Lewis, one Holman Projector and two Parachute and Cable rockets.

'At 1735, whilst lying at anchor (heading South East), an aircraft appeared off our port beam flying very low. When the aircraft was in range, we opened fire with our port bridge machine guns. The aircraft swerved towards the aft end of the ship, circled and flew across the Corsea, *which was lying at anchor ahead of us and had also opened fire as the aircraft approached. The aircraft swerved and dropped one bomb, doing no damage. The aircraft machine-gunned the* Corsea *as it approached but we were not machine-gunned. The aircraft then turned and went back towards the Tees.*

'At about 1745 an aircraft again approached from our port beam. I had everyone standing by the guns, as I had expected another attack. The plane was flying very low on the water but as he approached the bridge of the ship, he rose a little to clear our masts. We opened fire with our bridge machine guns and the aircraft banked and swerved towards the stern of the ship, dropping five bombs...'

Chief Steward John Cavanagh was manning the twin-Lewis gun on the port side of the bridge. When I tracked John down in Seaham Harbour in December 1997, he could remember only that *Empire Bay* had been waiting off Hartlepool for some time when the ship's crew heard the wail of Hartlepool's town siren, which, according to John, was *'..the only indication that a raid was a possibility..'*. Shortly afterwards, the members of the crew were called to action stations but it was some time before they heard the dull drone of aero engines.

'We heard the plane and it was not long before we saw it approaching us. I wanted to start shooting there and then but the captain, a veteran of the Dover Patrol in the First War, kept shouting: "Guns, hold your fire! Hold your fire!"

'The plane was getting bigger with the passing of every second as it flew towards us. I thought that it was going to hit us before we got the chance to fire. I think I'd have emptied my pan of ammunition before he'd reached us, had it been left to me. But, as it turned out, the captain

John Cavanagh, Chief Steward of the Empire Bay, *January 1942*
[John Cavanagh]

knew what he was doing...'

John said that the Dornier was 200 feet high when it flashed across the *Empire Bay* and dropped its bombs towards the steamer.

'It was so vivid. I could actually see the Germans in the plane. I could see them. Then we saw the bombs dropping and I fired about a 15-second burst at him as five or six bombs straddled the ship. I don't recall the aircraft strafing us. It might have done, but in the excitement and confusion — the twin-Lewis made quite a racket and there was the explosion of bombs and huge fountains of water — who knows?'

Captain Parks subsequently reported that of the five bombs aimed at the vessel:

'Four fell very close to the ship on the port side and appeared to be delayed action, as they did not explode until a little after striking the water. The fifth bomb fell close on the starboard quarter and there was a violent explosion that lifted the ship out of the water.

'When the aircraft was about 500 yards from the ship, I fired the port PAC rocket and I do not know whether it was the rocket or our machine gun fire that caused the aircraft to swerve. The gunner on the aft Hotchkiss fired three strips of ammunition into the aircraft and smoke was observed coming from one engine as it flew off. We did not see it again.'

Losing height and trailing a plume of black smoke, the enemy machine flew inland towards the Tees balloon cordon. Minutes later, it collided with the cable of a balloon flying 4,000 feet above Smith's Dock. The collision ripped a ten-foot length off the Dornier's starboard wing and virtually stopped the bomber in its tracks. Second later, the crushed remnants of the bomber's tangled wreckage were blazing ferociously on the railway sidings (OS.534213) of the steelworks of Dorman, Long & Co, at the bottom of Clay Lane and 100 yards east of what is now South Bank railway station, on the Darlington-

Saltburn line.

The airman in charge of No.35 Tees Barrage Balloon site (O.S. 531221), close by Smith's Tees Dockyard, was Leading Aircraftman Walter Myers, who now lives in Sedgefield, Co. Durham. In 1943, the Government's Ministry of Information booklet *Roof over Britain* (HMSO 1943) published Walter's version of the events that night.

LAC Walter Myèrs, who was in charge of No. 35 Balloon site on 15 January 1942. [Walter Myers]

'It was just getting dark when we got orders to fly our balloon. In a few minutes she was off the bed and aloft. We were rather pleased with ourselves, the boys and me, for we had put it up in extra quick time. I remember saying to one of our blokes, "If we don't get Annie up soon we'll probably be too late." I was only joking, really, because we had put our Annie up scores of times before without even hearing an enemy plane.

'Well, when she was up we trooped back to our hut, leaving the duty piquet on guard. We'd just started listening to the radio when we heard the plane coming low - very low, it was; much too low for my liking - so we decided to go outside and get a bit of cover. We'd no sooner got outside than the noise of the plane changed to a whine. It seemed as if it was diving right on top of us.

"Jenny Macke!" says one of our airmen, an Irishman who says things like that when he's roused. "Jenny Macke!" he says, "he's going to machine-gun us."

"No, he isn't," says I. "He's going to hit the cable." And he did. He went smack into it. There was a crash and the winch jumped as she took the strain. The cable sawed through the wing like a grocer's wire goes through cheese. That fixed him. Off came the best part of the starboard wing and we knew we'd got him.'

The ten-foot section of severed wing eventually fluttered to earth and landed a mile or so beyond where the Dornier crashed.

Mr C.V. Evans, warden of Grangetown Boys' Club, was in South Bank at the time and heard the plane travelling '..*very low and very fast*..'. When it collided with the cable, there was a yellow flash and the engine note immediately changed. His first thought was that South Bank was going to be dive-bombed, but he was mistaken. Clearly out of control, the Dornier screamed low over the housetops and then plunged into the coal sidings at Clay Lane, South Bank. It crashed at great speed with a thunderous roar and in a sheet of flame that momentarily turned night into day. The explosive force of the impact tore up 100 yards of railway track and made a hole some twelve feet deep. Then the wreck began to burn like a Brock's Benefit, its supply of Very cartridges popping off and arching skywards in a macabre fireworks' display. Instinctively, Evans ran towards the blazing wreck, but the heat was so intense that he could not get near. In any case, his was a futile gesture: the fliers were already beyond help. It took the firemen, from the NFS 'Action Station' in nearby Lorne Terrace, half an hour to quench the flames with foam.

The crash site was examined the next day by Air Ministry investigators. They found that most of the wreckage was buried in the crater and that the few fragments that were on the surface were burnt and of little Intelligence value. However, largely because the aircraft had dived on to an important double-track railway siding '*which was needed immediately for work of national importance*', they decided not to fully excavate the site but to repair the damage and reinstate the track as swiftly as possible. They did, however, retrieve one 13mm machine-gun as well as ammunition for 15mm and 20mm calibre weapons before the hole was filled in and a new track laid. Three badly burned corpses were also recovered from the wreck and were subsequently buried at the Acklam Road cemetery, Thornaby, under the names of Joachim Lehnis, Rudolf Matern and Heinrich Richter. The body of the fourth member, believed at the time to be that of radio-operator Hans Maneke, was not found.

Leutnant Rudolf Matern , the observer of Do.217 U5+HS.
[via Kurt Matern]

It might well be that the Dornier was not the only Luftwaffe loss over the Tees that night for the Hartlepool lifeboat crew spent three hours searching Tees Bay after a score of red and white distress signals were seen by Observer Corps and coast-watchers. At the time, it was generally believed that the signals were discharged by downed aircrew, but it was a wild

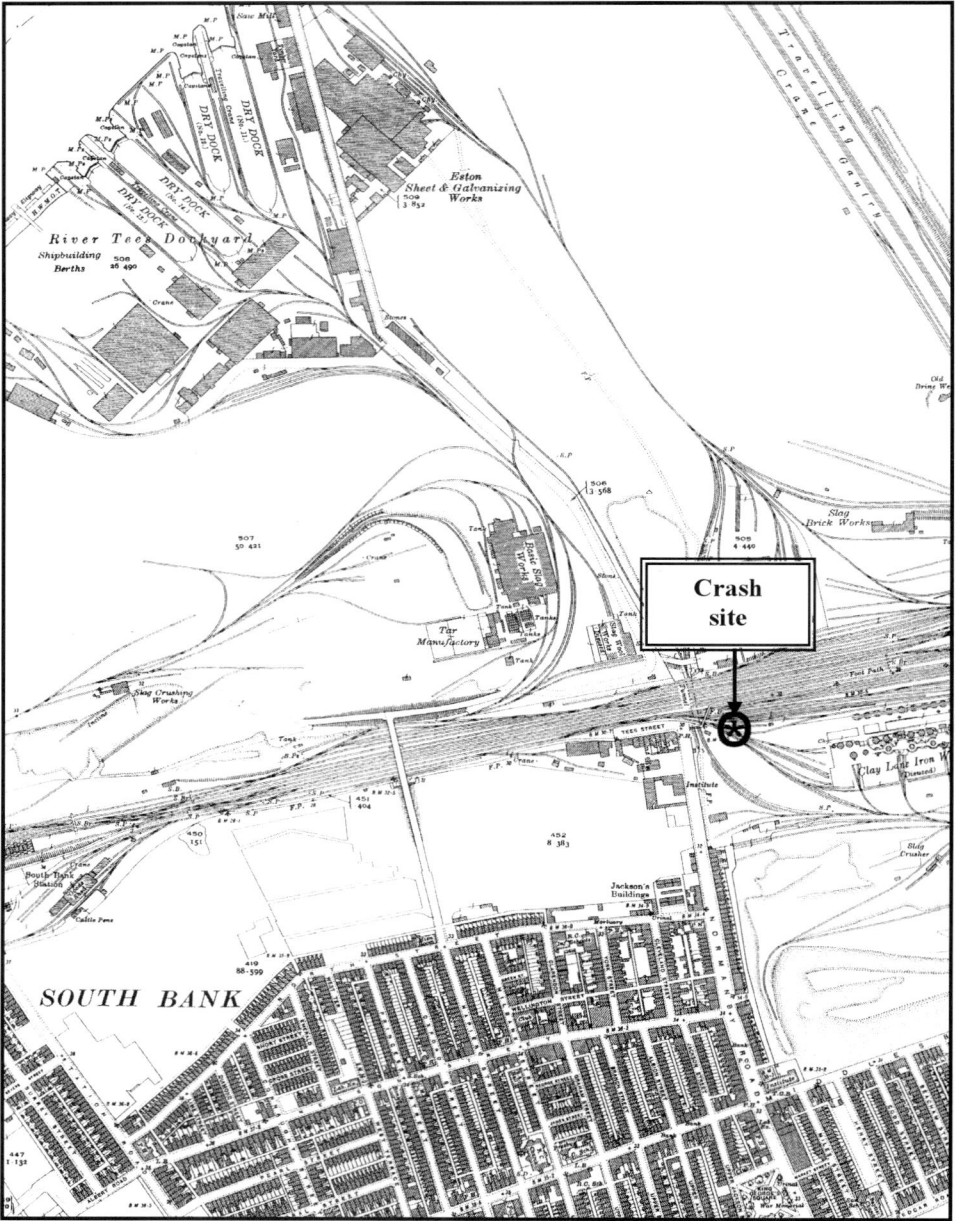

Crash
site

Crown copyright 1927

14

16 January 1942. The Dornier crash site at South Bank [Courtesy of The Northern Echo]

'.Seemingly, there was very little wreckage above the ground and most of that was burnt.. ' [Courtesy of The Northern Echo]

night and there was a high sea running. The search yielded nothing. If the flares had been fired by aircrew in distress then men and machines must have sunk without trace. The crew of the *Empire Bay* had better luck.

Fifty-six years on, John Cavanagh could not remember whether the bombs had actually hit his ship but he believes that they certainly exploded close enough to rupture the sides of the vessel. The damage would eventually sink her, but that final event was destined to take some hours. *Empire Bay* settled first by the stern, the raised bow held high by the anchor chain, and hung there for quite a while until the increasing weight of water within the hull finally began to ease the ship below the waves. As evening wore on, it became increasingly clear that there could be only one outcome. At 7.30pm, as the balloon crew set about their task of replacing their charge, the Tees pilot cutter *W.R. Lister* slipped her moorings to answer an urgent appeal for assistance from the crippled steamer. A contemporary report of the incident by Pilot W.H. 'Bill' Young, the duty skipper of the cutter, described what happened.

'The vessel had been bombed and seriously damaged. The Empire Bay *was sinking, but we were unaware of this fact. To locate the ship without lights under such conditions was a trying affair. Moreover, the cutter performed every gyration short of capsizing. After thirty minutes of steaming, a flame was sighted away to northward. The course was altered and shortly afterwards we came upon* Empire Bay *plunging to her anchor and awash from quarter to poop. The Hartlepool and Tees*

Do.217 U5+KS (wnr 4378) of 8./KG2 belonged to the same Staffel as the 'South Bank' Dornier. It is hard to imagine that so much of an aircraft of this size lay buried in the hole shown on p16. [via Manfred Griehl]

Examination vessel was in the vicinity and she contacted us by loud-hailer. She informed us that she considered it unsafe to launch either of her boats but that she would be willing to give us plenty of light by means of her searchlights if we intended any rescue. This we readily took advantage of and closed the Empire Bay *on her starboard quarter very cautiously.*

'After one or two determined attempts to wreck herself among the upturned boats, rafts, fathoms of lifeboat falls, and empty davits swinging drunkenly outboard, the cutter was coaxed alongside the quickly settling vessel. We were now on the starboard side, which was swept continuously by heavy seas, lifting and falling, crashing and jarring. But one by one the men jumped and fell aboard the cutter. Soon they were safely aboard and, making them as comfortable as limited accommodation permitted, we proceeded towards the Tees' entrance.

'During the whole of the operation I was ably assisted by Tees pilots C. Gray, G. Pounder and J.C. Swinburne and my crew, including the engineer and apprentices Franklin and Cook'.

III. / Kampfgeschwader 2

Lfd. Nr.	Ort u. Tag des Berluftes	Staffel ufw.	Dienftgrad	Borname	Familienname, Truppenteil Nr. der Erkennungsmarke	Geburts-		
						Tag	Ort	Kreis
1	2	3	4	5	6	7	8	9
1.	ostw.Middles-brough. 15.1.1942 17.30 Uhr Do 217 E-4	8.	Feldw. aktiv F	Joachim	L e h n i s 8./K.G. 2 69 642 32	18. 8. 18	Danzig	
2.	Werk-Nr. 5314	8.	Leutnant d.R. B	Rudolf	M a t e r n 8./K.G. 2 58 209 15	20. 8. 17	Paderbo *Westfal.* *Ind.*	
3.		8.	Uffz. d.R. BF	Hans	M a n e k e 8./K.G. 2 57 359 75	26. 4. 18	Berli.. Tegel	
4.		8.	Ofw. aktiv BM	Heinric'	R i c h t e r 8./K.G. 2 7. U.G. 3 63	16. 7. 11	Herisch-dorf Kr. Hirsch-berg *Niederschl.*	

The Luftwaffe Namenverlustmeldung (Loss reports by name) *records the loss of Lehnis and his crew East of Middlesbrough on 15 January 1942.* [Author's collection]

H.Piper. Oblt　　　　31.1.42
and Squadron Commander

Dear Mr Richter,

As your son Heinrich's squadron commander I must unfortunately give this sad notification that your son did not return from an operation against England on 15.1.42 and has been missing since then. His crew had orders to attack in the early evening a convoy on the English East coast.

Unfortunately there was no radio contact with the aircraft so we have no explanation for its failure to return. Therefore it remains only a hope that the crew have been taken into English captivity. However, it can take up to two months until we receive confirmation.

For you now comes a time of waiting, hoping and uncertainty regarding the fate of your son and I also know that this is very hard. But you should and must always find consolation in the thought that your son fought in our mighty and glorious Luftwaffe and was completely loyal to his soldier's oath and, until the last, had a grand objective—the liberation of our Fatherland. What he can longer accomplish, we will accomplish!

I have already notified your daughter-in-law.

Yours sincerely and Heil Hitler.
Hubertus Piper (signed)
Oberleutnant.

Sad news is bad news in any language. The above letter was sent to the Richter family by Oberleutnant Hubertus Piper, the CO of 8./KG2. I do wonder whether the Richter family found the rather strident political overtones a comfort at, what must have been, a very difficult time for them. [via Werner Feige]

Tees' Pilot Bill Young (above) and the pilot cutter W.R. Lister *in which he and others went to the aid of* Empire Bay *on the night of 15 January 1942.*   [Author's collection]

The matter-of-fact nature of this report belies the drama of the situation—and the danger that men were willing to face in order to go to the aid of strangers in distress. It was not a new phenomenon: others had performed similar acts before and others would do so afterwards. As it happened, the *Empire Bay* incident proved to be one of the most notable rescue feats effected by Tees pilots during the war years: it appears to have passed virtually unnoticed.

John Cavanagh and his shipmates were landed ashore and spent the night at a local hospital, largely for observation purposes.
'While we were there we heard that Annie *the balloon had got her first victim, but it was ours. Mind you, it didn't really matter who got the credit. We'd survived and the plane was down, that was the main thing.'*

The *Empire Bay* sank later that evening. In 1946, the vessel was dispersed to the sea bed by the Admiralty Wreck Disposal Organisation. Much of the wreck was still in tact in 1988, when it lay at 54°41'08"N/01°08'36"W at a depth of fifteen metres.

Following the 're-discovery' of the wreck on 27 November 1997, a full excavation of the site by a team of Royal Engineers from No. 33 Explosive Ordnance Disposal Unit, Wimbish, working with specialists from No. 5131 Bomb Disposal Squadron, RAF Wittering, ultimately yielded some five tons of wreckage, including a large quantity of small arms ammunition, a number

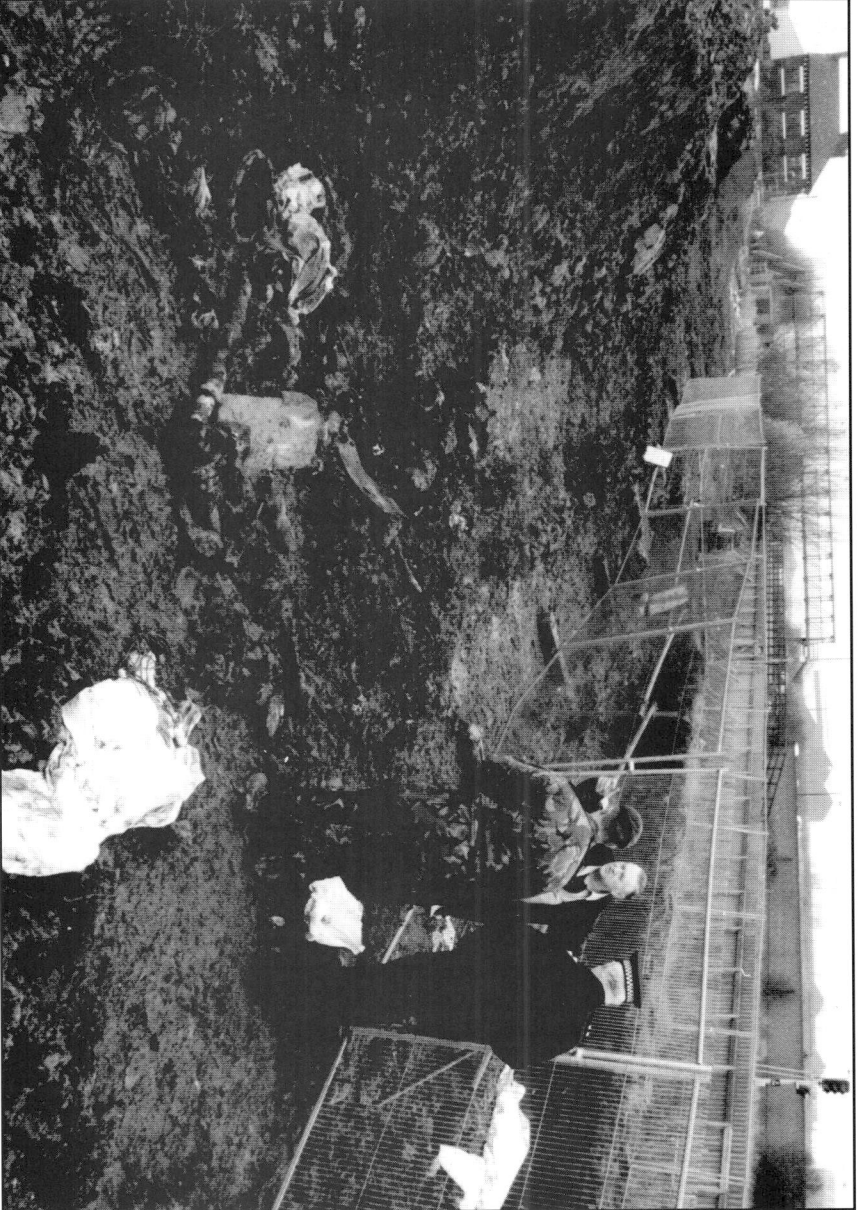

27 November 1997. The crash site prior to the main excavation. The patches of white are parachutes, opened for the first time in fifty-five years by the workers who made the initial discovery. [Author]

Dornier 217E-4 Bomber

A Dornier 217E-4 (F8+BM; wnr 4381) of 4./KG40, showing the positions that would have been occupied by the 'South Bank' crew on the 15 January 1942: **1**. Joachim Lehnis (pilot); **2**. Hans Maneke (radio-operator/gunner); **3**. Rudolf Matern (observer/bomb-aimer); **4**. Heinrich Richter (mechanic/ gunner).

Powered by two BMW 801C engines, the Do.217E-4 had a maximum speed of 550 km/h (342mph) without a payload, and 450km/h (280mph) fully loaded. Its armament consisted of 1 x 13mm MG131 gun in the electrically operated dorsal turret; 1 x 13mm MG131 gun in the ventral position; 1 x 20mm cannon and 1 x 15mm MG 151 cannon in the nose; and 1 x 7.9mm twin MG81 on each side of the cockpit. Whenever this type of aircraft raided northern England, it operated from bases in Holland and usually carried a bomb load of 4 x 500kg high explosive bombs *or* 2 x 500kg and 1 x 1,200kg high explosive bombs *or* 1,000 x 2kg fire-bombs. Thus the bomb load for the operation on 15 January seems to have been an exception to the rule, if Captain Parks was correct in his assessment. Do.217E-4s operating against England usually had balloon-cable cutters fitted to the leading edge of the wings—which makes one wonder why the 'South Bank' machine was brought down in the way that it was.

The aircraft shown above was lost on a mine-laying sortie on the night of 4/5 January 1943, when it flew into a Sussex hillside at 350 feet and crashed through an empty bungalow. All four members of the crew were killed.

[photograph via Willi Schludecker]

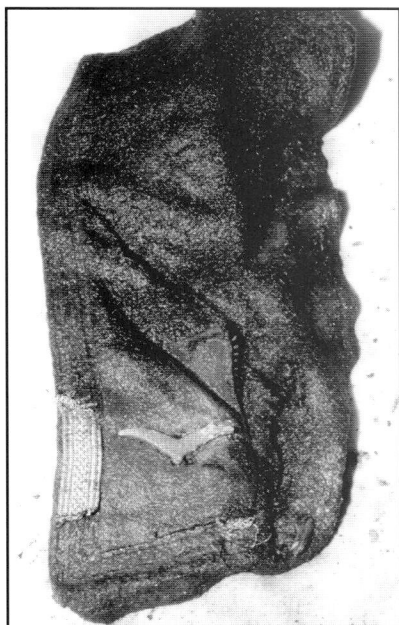

A fragment of Hans Maneke's uniform. [via M. Coverdale]

of machine-guns, two parachutes in surprisingly good condition, a wooden propeller, parts of the undercarriage (oleo legs and wheel) and parts of the fuselage.

The discovery of fragments of a battledress collar and a small number of human bones quite early in the investigation gave rise to the belief that the fourth member of the crew had been in the Dornier when it crashed. The fact that the collar bore the rank insignia (one eagle) of an Unteroffizier seemed to confirm that the remains were those of Hans Maneke, the only member of the crew with that rank and the only one without a headstone in Thornaby cemetery.

However, a measure of confusion was introduced when other, more substantial, human remains were unearthed much deeper in the excavation and close by what would have been the ventral gunner's position. The discovery of part of a Luftwaffe battledress blouse bearing the collar insignia of three eagles near the remains led investigators to speculate that the remains were those of the pilot, Feldwebel Joachim Lehnis. However, following some inspired speculation by my friend Peter Kirk, of Derby, subsequent forensic examination revealed that a fourth eagle was missing from the insignia, which meant that the wearer had held the rank of Oberfeldwebel. A coroner's inquest, held on Teesside in June 1998, therefore concluded that the remains were those of the ventral gunner, Oberfeldwebel Heinrich Richter, and pointed to a confusion of identities half a century earlier, Maneke having been buried under Richter's name in 1942. That error was corrected on 13 October 1998, when Hans Maneke's grave was marked with a new headstone and that of Richter was removed pending its relocation over the new grave.

The following day, after a service in a South Bank church packed to capacity, Heinrich Richter was buried alongside his comrades at Thornaby. Among those present were the German Consul-General to Britain, the German Air Attaché, three local mayors, the representatives of twenty-two ex-Serviceman's associations and some two hundred members of the general public. Attempts by the German authorities to trace surviving relatives of

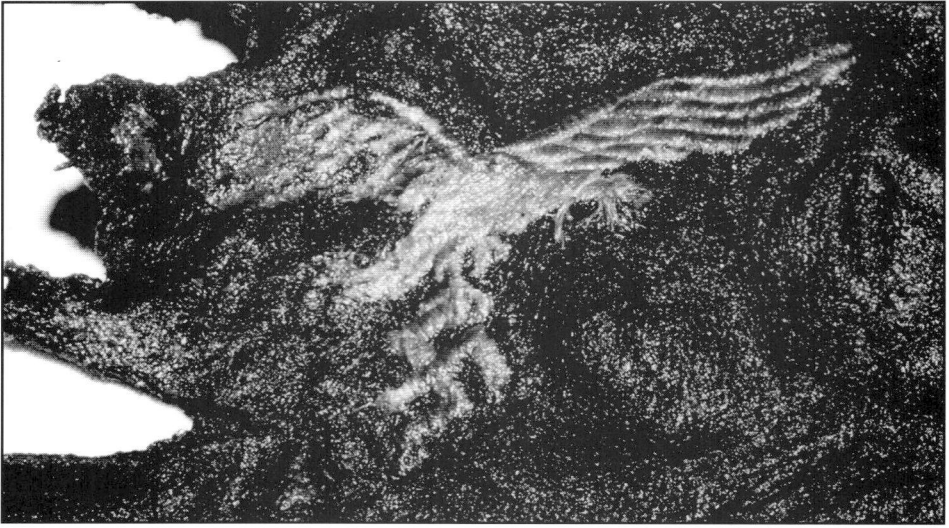

The Luftwaffe eagle emblem on a piece of badly oil-stained battle dress retrieved from the wreck. [via M. Coverdale]

'The discovery of part of a Luftwaffe battledress blouse bearing the collar insignia of three eagles near the remains led investigators to speculate that the remains were those of the pilot, Feldwebel Joachim Lehnis. However, subsequent forensic examination revealed that a fourth eagle was missing from the badge of rank....A coroner's inquest..therefore concluded that the remains were those of ventral gunner Oberfeldwebel Heinrich Richter...'
[via M. Coverdale]

Richter and Maneke had met with no success but among those present was Heinz Möllenbrok, a former Dornier 17 pilot of KG2 who had been shot down during the Battle of Britain, and who had travelled from Germany to represent the KG2 Association. He laid the first wreath on Richter's grave. Then he placed a garlanded wreath of poppies on the grave of a British flier, in recognition of the 55,000 members of RAF Bomber Command who had failed to return from operations during the Second World War.

The number of local people who attended the burial ceremony and the church service that preceded it made a distinct impression on Heinz Möllenbrok and on Hans Mondorf, the German Consul-General. Addressing the funeral congregation at St. Peter's Church, South Bank (the nearest church to the crash site), Herr Mondorf said:

'I was quite moved and surprised by the sympathy that this case attracted with the population here. I have travelled very long distances in Europe. It is not uncommon still to have hatred towards former enemies, especially towards Germans. This is understandable, particularly in countries where the Germans had been in occupation; where people suffered from the Gestapo and SS. It is not the case here. I attribute this attitude to the sense of fair play which the British soul enshrines. Let us honour all of those who tragically lost their lives

14 October 1998. The burial of Heinrich Richter at Thornaby cemetery. Heinz Möllenbrok, representing the KG2 Old Comrades Association, stands middle right holding the garlanded wreath.. [Stuart McMillan]

A bugler of Cleveland Police sounds the Last Post....

...and Standards are lowered.
[Both photographs by Stuart McMillan]

during this cruel war. Let's hope that nothing similar ever happens again'.

At the graveside, seventy-eight year-old Heinz Möllenbrok voiced similar sentiments when he appealed for the spirit of reconciliation to continue through future generations.   For me, at least, that spirit was amply demonstrated by an elderly lady who came forward to place her own small bouquet of flowers after the official wreaths had been laid. It transpired that she had been a member of the Belgian Resistance when her country had been under German occupation during the last war. Her husband of two weeks had been shot by the Gestapo. In those dangerous days, she had not been able to place flowers on her husband's grave but, she said, she hoped that someone had done so on her behalf.

Local legend has it that some time after the cessation of hostilities in 1945, a German lady visited South Bank and sought the location of the crash site. It is said that she told people that her son had been one of the crew of the Dornier but that he had never been found. If the story is true, the lady must have been the mother of Hans Maneke, for by then the radio-operator's three colleagues had been given headstones in Thornaby cemetery. Sadly, she could not have known that an error had been made; and if she visited Thornaby and stood by the graves of her son's friends, she would not have known that she was standing within six feet of her child.

There were no members of Heinrich Richter's family present when he was buried on 14 October 1998, and it seems that any trace of Frau Maneke was lost long ago. However, they were represented on the day—by a grey-haired old lady who had refuted justifiable reasons to feel bitter and whose spontaneous floral tribute made a far deeper impression on many of those present than did the impressive, and faultless, official arrangements. It was moving moment.

A further seven years were to pass before any relatives of Heinrich Richter visited his grave in Thornaby cemetery. It subsequently transpired that although the news of the discovery and subsequent re-burial of Richter's remains was given wide coverage in Britain, it was given very little publicity in the German media. Thus, his relatives in Germany were unaware of the events in England. However, in April 1999, a short article about those events appeared in *Schlesische Bergwacht*, an expatriate newspaper for Germans who had formerly lived in Silesia (now a province of Poland) and had been forced to move to Germany in the immediate post-war years. Heinrich Richter and his family were of Silesian origin and his surviving relatives still take the newspaper.

When Richter's nephew, Werner Feige, read the article, he was certain that the report concerned his uncle, even though the article stated that the German airman had 'no known relatives'. The letter he then wrote to the newspaper was published a week or so later and brought him into contact with the man who would complete the circle. Shortly after the publication of Werner's letter, he was contacted by Gotthard Liebich, himself a Silesian expatriate, who had been captured in Normandy in 1944 and who had settled in England after the war. Liebich had been on the trail of Richter's family ever since his friend, Heinz Möllenbrok, had told him about the events in England. It was Möllenbrok who had provided Gotthard Liebich with much of the information relating to Richter and it was Liebich who passed that information on to the family and arranged the visit to Teesside. Two months later, using a combination of 1942 Luftwaffe documentation and the Internet, I found Rudolf Matern's brother living in Paderborn.

As far as I know, Matern's brother has never visited Thornaby but members of the Richter family came to Teesside in April 2005. During the visit, Werner Feige told me that the family had been informed in January 1942 that Richter and his crew had failed to return from operations over England but that it was hoped that they had survived as prisoners of war. By April 1942, that hope had faded and the family was informed that the crew must be presumed to be dead. It was the last information they received about the matter. Werner Feige went on to explain:

'When Herr Liebich showed us the many newspaper reports from England, we were all very impressed and moved, but we were terribly disappointed that the German media would not touch the subject. Honouring a soldier in Germany is taboo. My mother had three brothers and all of them were killed in the war. One was killed in Russia in October 1941. Three months later, Heinrich was lost over

England. And the youngest brother was listed as "Missing in Action" in 1944. We found out in 1972 that he had been lost in Romania.

'When we learned that our uncle was buried in England, we saw it as our duty to make the effort to visit. We are deeply moved to visit our uncle's grave. Our only regret is that our mother and Heinrich's other sister's are not alive to witness this.'

16 April 2005. Members of the Feige family at Thornaby cemetery with friends Eva Yarrow (2nd from left) and Gotthard Liebich (1st from right). [Author]

Heinrich Richter (centre) with his brothers Gerhard (left) and Kurt (right). All three were killed in the Second World War. Gerhard Richter was killed in Rumania in August 1944 and Kurt in Russia in October 1941. [via Werner Feige]

Obfw. Heinrich Richter and his grave at Acklam Road cemetery, Thornaby. [via Werner Feige and author respectively]

Postscript

When I first researched this incident in 1990, I was of the opinion that Lehnis and his crew might have been responsible for dropping two bombs on Skinningrove Ironworks at about 5.30pm on 15 January 1942, prior to engaging the steamer *Empire Bay* [see *Luftwaffe over the North* (1993)]. However, since then evidence has emerged that shows beyond doubt that Ju88s of *Kampfgruppe 506* (also detailed with KG2 to attack the convoy) were responsible for the bombing of the ironworks. The *Kampfgruppe 506* Operations Record Book (*Kriegstagebuch*) shows that Ju88 S4+AL of *Kampfstaffel 3./506* dropped 1x SC1200kg bomb and 1x SC500kg bomb from an altitude of forty metres at 5.30pm (BST) and claimed hits on a blast-furnace, a coking plant and on rolling mills, while at 5.32pm a second Ju88 (unidentified but probably S4+LK of 2./506) dropped two more bombs, which failed to explode. The subsequent works' assessment reported damage to the boilers, the soaking pits and several buildings, as well to the water mains and cooling services. Although the damage was not extensive in scale, it was thought at the time that it might have a serious effect on production. Eleven workers were injured in the attack, two of whom (Mr A.W.Smith and Mr W.G. Lewis) required hospitalisation.

It was not the first time that aircraft targeted against shipping had chosen to attack land targets instead.. The practice of anti-shipping patrols substituting a 'safer' target when met with strong maritime anti-aircraft defence occurred on a number of occasions along the coastal areas of North-east England and small ports like Bridlington, Scarborough and Whitby—as well the ironworks at Skinningrove and Warrenby—were all subjected to such 'visits' at one time or another.

One of the four Ju88s that set out from Leeuwarden was lost on this operation when S4+EH (wnr..1612) of 1./506 came down off Tynemouth. Its crew of Unteroffizier Friedrich Pott (pilot), Leutnant zur See Dieter Andresen (observer/bomb-aimer), Unteroffizier Josef Scholze (radio-operator/ gunner) and Feldwebel Franz Hruschake

Hylton cemetery, Sunderland. [Author]

(mechanic/gunner) did not survive but only the body of Dieter Andresen was ever found. It was recovered from Priors Haven, Tynemouth, on 27 January 1942 and was buried at Hylton Cemetery, Sunderland, some days later.

There is a possibility that S4+EH fell to anti-aircraft fire from 'C' Troop, 278 LAA Bty, 68 LAA Regt. RA. Alan White, of Houghton-le-Spring (Co. Durham) believes that the unit, of which his father was a member, was credited with the shooting down of Andresen's aircraft and that they were awarded a Troop cup (engraved *16* January 1942) to mark their success. Alan's claim has yet to be confirmed.

Members of 'C' Troop, 278 LAA Bty, 68 LAA Regt. RA [via Alan White]

Pte Thomas White. [via Alan White]

The 'C' Troop cup. [via Alan White]

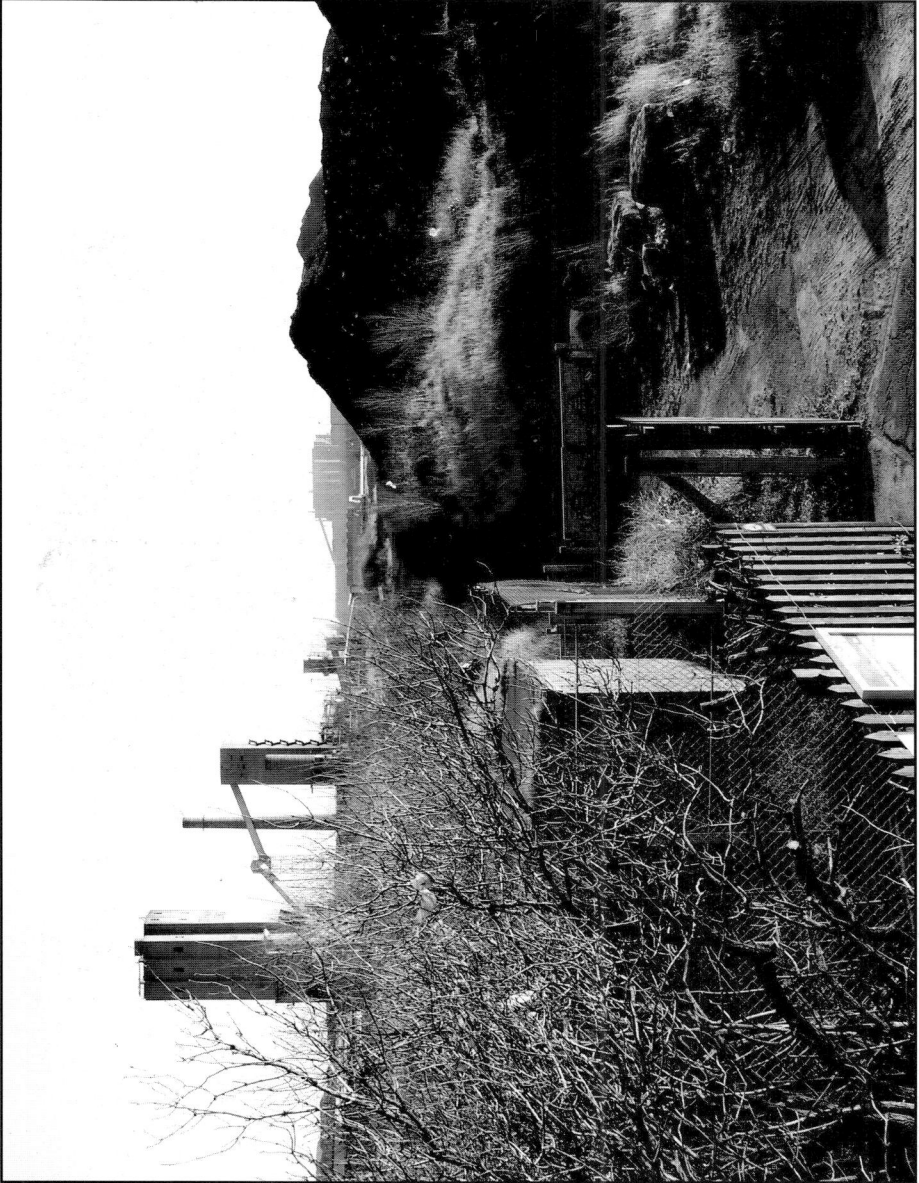

The crash site as it was on 30 January 2008. The business park development is to the right, beyond the earth mounds. [Author]

Respect for a former enemy

Like any member of the armed forces of any country who knowingly puts himself in danger, Heinrich Richter was a brave man. A veteran of campaigns in Poland, the Low Countries and against the United Kingdom, he had flown at least sixty war flights (for which he had been awarded the *Frontflugspange* in Silver) and in so doing had exposed himself to personal danger each time his aircraft left the ground; he had previously been wounded in action (for which he had been awarded the Wound Badge) before his fateful flight over Teesside; and he was the holder of the Iron Cross First Class and the Iron Cross Second Class. And he knew that, unlike his RAF counterparts, there was no set number of operations after the completion of which he would be rested.; he knew that he would have to continue flying until he was either killed, wounded or injured to such an extent that operational flying was no longer an option. One might not agree with the political ideology he represented, whether he subscribed to it or not, but one cannot fail to respect his courage

The funeral of Heinrich Richter was widely reported in this country, both in the press and on television. There was much less coverage in Germany, where publicity for veterans of the Second World War is far more muted and where, as Werner Feige says, *'honouring a soldier is taboo'*. That seems to be the case with regard to *all* German veterans of the Second World War and not just those who gained an infamous reputation for atrocities committed on an unimaginable scale. The 'honourable' and the 'dishonourable' among those who served appear to have been indiscriminately 'lumped' together in the post-war German psyche and are now virtually indistinguishable—much to the chagrin of those non-politically motivated ex-soldiers who feel that they had simply attempted to serve their country in its hour of need and had tried to do so fairly and within the accepted rules of conventional warfare. They see themselves as ordinary men who did a job which, at the time, seemed necessary and they feel betrayed by the fact that the public mood in post-war Germany does not recognise that.

Ironically, recognition of the wartime service of 'honourable' German soldiers has often come from the direction least expected: from former 'enemies' who shared with them the bloody conflicts of sixty-odd years ago. Witness, for example, the many British war veterans in attendance, and the number of ex-servicemen's standards on parade, at

Richter's funeral; standards borne by men who had answered *their* country's call and had done what they perceived to have been *their* duty. Among them was D-Day veteran John Armstrong, 83, who saw action with the Sixth Airborne Division. Perhaps he spoke for all of the veterans present when he said:

'Richter was only doing a job, as we were. Why should he not be afforded the same service as anyone else?'

Consul-General Hans Mondorf was not the only German to acknowledge Teesside's generosity of spirit in the case of Richter. I know that John Armstrong's sentiments certainly struck a cord with former KG2 pilot Heinz Möllenbrok. Letters written by former-Luftwaffe fliers living in Germany and shown below bear witness to the fact that Teesside's gesture was also appreciated elsewhere.

Letters of Appreciation

Former Luftwaffe Unteroffizier Otto Linsner flew Ju.25 tri-motor transport aircraft in Europe, Russia and the Middle East before being captured in North Africa. He sent two letters to the *Evening Gazette* after receiving a number of press cuttings relating to the funeral from his friend Heinz Möllenbrok. His first letter was published on 17 November 1998, the second one on 29 December 1998.
(see next page)

Uffz Otto Linsner in 1941.
[Otto Linsner]

Dear Sir,

A friend of mine sent me your article about the funeral of Heinrich Richter at South Bank.

As a former Transportflyer, Junkers 52, I was very moved with the honour and respect shown by the people of South Bank in Middlesbrough, and the veterans, who paid tribute to a former bomber flyer of the German air force. It was very honourable to see veterans take down their flags when the body of Richter was lowered into the grave; British soldiers with caps and medals and their flags. I am so thankful for it.

I am in good comradeship with many British veterans, especially of the Army Veterans Association.

Once more, thank you for all you have done for my German DO17 comrades.

Otto Linsner.
Wiesbaden, Germany.

Dear Sir

First of all, thank you so much that you had published my letter about the funeral of Heinrich Richter, the airman who was killed when his plane crashed at South Bank during the Second World War.

I had a talk with the editor of our *Rhein-Main-News*. I asked if he would publish your article, and he has done so. I am so glad that in this area of Germany people can read it; that our former 'enemies' are honourable humans.

England has done it. Germany has not done it. My letters to our governments and politicians were in vain. So I have found an Editor who has published it. I'm so thankful. I think our politicians can learn something from you. Thank you, England.

I wish you, all your Evening Gazette staff and readers, all people and old veterans who have given my comrade of DO17 the last respects, health and luck for the next year 1999.

Otto Linsner.
Wiesbaden, Germany

Klaus J. Scheer
Rechtsanwalt

Privat. Grosshesseloher Str. 19
81479 Munchen-Solln
Telefon 089. 790 19 88
Telefax 089. 790 08 63

April 1oth, 1999

To the Mayor of
South Bank/England

Dear Mr. Mayor,

the striking article in the Times of 15.1o.1998 "Britons
pay final Tribute to German pilot" got to my knowledge through
reprint by the "Jägerblatt", a publication of the veteran pilot

We all were impressed, how your community and the British
veterans honoured this pilot, who lost his life during the war
over England. I come from the same village as Heinrich Richter,
Herischdorf close to Hirschberg in Silesia, and naturally gave
this news to my former classmates and to a paper "Schlesische
Bergwacht", whose readers formerly lived in this eastern part
of Germany, which now is Polish. The first reaction came from
a former neigbour of Heinrich Richter and a few days ago the
news had reached a family member, Werner Feige, a nephew of
Heinrich Richter. For the family this was the first news about
the fate of him, who had lived until now with the letter of his
unit "missed in action".

Heinrich Richter , born 1911, was trained to be a technician
in a company which produced machines to make paper. He had
two brothers, unfortunately all three were killed in action
during the war.

Being a former nightfighterpilot myself, I would like to thank
you and your community and especially the veterans like
Walter Myers, the former commander of the balloon unit, on
behalf of the family of Heinrich Richter, his friends of his
homevillage and last not least on behalf of all the former
airforce pilots, who all felt deeply touched and honoured
by this great gesture of your British countrymen.

Sincerely yours,

Klaus J. Scheer,

The above is a letter of appreciation to the Mayor of South Bank from a wartime Luftwaffe night-fighter pilot who had read a report of the funeral in the British newspaper The Times. *[via Werner Feige]*

A bizarre ending to tragic tales?

When the funeral was over and small and large 'knots' of strangers stood around the graveyard conversing about a man they had never known, Valerie and Jim Edon, of Colby Newham, announced to a TV reporter that they believed that their son Carl had been a reincarnation of Heinrich Richter. Carl had died in 1995 but his parents believed that in attending the funeral of the German airman they had, in fact, witnessed the burial of their son for a second time.

Carl Edon was born in 1972 and was the youngest of three children but, according to his mother, 'he looked nothing like his brother or sister.' It seems that he acted quite differently from them too. His parents explained that from an early age he claimed that in a previous life he had been a pilot in the German air force. From the age of three he told of being surrounded by glass while flying an aircraft; he told of the time that his aircraft crashed and one of his legs had been broken; and he claimed that, later on, he had been killed when his plane had crashed during a raid on England.

Though initially dismissed as childhood imaginings, Carl's 'recollections' persisted and, with the passing of time, were extended. It is said that at a later age he recalled seeing Hitler at Nuremburg; that he was able to describe in detail the Luftwaffe uniform and its insignia, and that on occasion he drew detailed drawings of aircraft cockpits. All of this, according to his father, without his seeing books that might have given him the necessary information. His parents also mention that Carl preferred the music of Bach and Strauss to the 'Pop' preferences of his contemporaries. They offered all of this as evidence of a life lived in a different age.

The impression that Carl made was such that when he was nine years old he was the subject of an article in the *Evening Gazette* and authors Peter and Mary Harrison devoted a chapter to his case in their book, *The Children That Time Forgot* (1989). The 'notoriety' these reports produced among pupils at Carl's school made him a figure of fun and, after that, his claims became less public—though it seems that he never stopped believing that he had once flown with the Luftwaffe.

In 1988, at the age of sixteen, Carl started work on the railway. Subsequently, he settled down with his childhood sweetheart and they had a child. By the summer of 1995, there was another child on the way. One could say that he had everything to live for. However, on 2

August 1995, when he was at the Grangetown railyard off Tees Dock Road, he was stabbed to death during a fight with a workmate. He was later buried at Acklam Road cemetery, Thornaby. A little over two years later, Richter's mortal remains were uncovered just a few hundred yards from where Carl Edon had died. It was enough to convince Valerie and Jim Edon that Heinrich Richter and their son had been one and the same.

Personally, I do not subscribe to the idea. I tend to believe that selective memory can be wedded to coincidence in order to produce any result one wants and then the product of imagination becomes 'reality'. Having said that, a year or so after Richter's funeral I established contact with members of his family in Germany. Among the photographs they sent to me was one of Heinrich recovering from an injury to his right leg—and another in which he bears a striking resemblance to Carl Edon. For his parents, the similarity was the final proof and the *Evening Gazette* was sufficiently impressed to give the story full page prominence on 15 January 2002, the sixtieth anniversary of the crash.

As for me, I still remain more than a little agnostic—and, for the time being, at least, I view the similarity of appearance simply as a further example of several strange (but impressive) coincidences.

Obfw. Heinrich Richter
[Werner Feige]

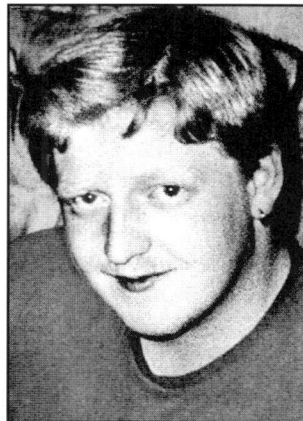

Carl Edon. [Mrs. V Edon]

The man who laid the first wreath:
Heinz Möllenbrok.

Heinz Möllenbrok (right) and Philipp Hess flying a Heinkel 111 prior to joining 3./KG2.
[via Heinz Möllenbrok]

Heinz-Georg Möllenbrok was born in Westphalia, northern Germany, in April 1920, and was the son of forester. He took an early interest in flying and was already a qualified glider pilot by the time he joined the Luftwaffe in November 1938. He undertook pilot training on the single-engine Focke-Wulf 44 'Stieglitz' and was awarded his wings in October 1939. Further training was successfully completed on multi-engine aircraft, including the Junkers 52, Junkers 86, Heinkel 111 and the Dornier 17. He was promoted to the rank of Leutnant in April 1940 and in the following June was posted to 3./KG2, an operational Dornier 17 bomber unit based at Epinoy, near Cambrai, in northern France. His crew was Unteroffizier Philipp Hess (observer/bomb-aimer), Gefreiter Gerhard Reineke (radio-operator/gunner) and Obergefreiter Johann Golob (mechanic/gunner).

By August 1940 they had flown at least six operations. These included two attacks on Channel shipping, two attacks on Folkestone and raids on airfields at Hawkinge and Lympe. At that time, the Battle of Britain was at its height and the skies over Kent were particularly dangerous for participants of

Ltn. Möllenbrok in 1940.
[Heinz Möllenbrok]

any nationality. On the afternoon of 16 August 1940, Möllenbrok and his crew discovered just *how* dangerous things could be.

In late afternoon of 16 August 1940, Heinz and his crew were flying one of the thirty-six Dornier 17Z bombers of I./KG2 that had been targeted against the RAF fighter station at Hornchurch, east of London. Under fighter escort, the formation crossed the Channel at 16,500 feet and was subjected to heavy AA fire over the Kent coast before being intercepted by fighters The Do.17(coded U5+LL) of 20-year-old Möllenbrok was the lead aircraft of the last three in the formation. None of them was to survive the encounter with Hurricanes of No.56 Squadron, North Weald. Heinz told me:

'We were attacked a number of times near Canterbury. On the first attack, the Dornier on my left was heavily hit and veered away past us. My Observer, Philip Hess, saw the machine swing away under us and recognised it as that of Oberleutnant Brandenburg. Probably the bomb load had not been jettisoned because the aircraft exploded and crashed near Whitstable. The crew of Oblt Brandenburg could not be individually identified and were buried as 'unidentified' in Whitstable cemetery. They were reburied at Cannock Chase in 1962.

'We received three or four attacks, during which two of my crew— Reineke and Golob—were either badly wounded or killed. During the first attack, we were wounded by a cone of bullets. Our right motor fell out, so that controlling the aircraft became difficult and keeping it in trim took all of my concentration. The rest of the Gruppe was flying above us by then and we were on our own as a straggler. At that time, behind me I could hear that Gerhard Reineke was still firing .

'The attacks continued and our 2cm cannon was used whenever a Hurricane or Spitfire passed in front of us. During the third or fourth attack a fighter came in front of us from below. Philip Hess fired at it with the 2cm cannon. The fighter must have been hit and I learned more recently that a Hurricane was later reported as having been shot down. Then my right arm was badly shattered and I was wounded in the shoulder, had a shell splinter in my lung and injuries to my head and to both legs. Consequently, I had even more difficulty maintaining control of the aircraft. Despite my wounded arm, for a short while I

was still able to steer the aircraft until, finally, another Hurricane came in from the front and our machine took more hits but we damaged that plane. Then a severe hit wrecked the steering mechanism. The steering column fell from my hands and the Dornier, on fire and riddled with bullet holes, was spiralling down. We had to evacuate the aircraft. 'Out! Out!' I shouted. Philipp Hess jettisoned our twenty 50kg bombs. I hope they did no damage.

'On looking back, I saw that the aircraft entrance hatch was already open and so I reasoned that Golob and Reineke had already left the aircraft. Believing that Golob and Reineke had already jumped, Hess and I went to get out but it became very difficult for us to leave the plane because of the spinning. Then suddenly Hess and I were sliding together through the hatch of the spiralling Dornier. But then we became jammed, half in and half out of the aircraft. I thought that we were firmly jammed by our parachutes but then Hess realised that our oxygen bottles had become hooked on the rim of the hatch. I could do nothing because of my badly wounded arm and I saw death definitely approaching.

'The engines were making a terrible screaming noise and the Dornier dropped from 4,000 metres to 1,000 metres before Hess managed by force to release us. Then suddenly all was quiet: I was free. With my left hand, I only just managed to pull the parachute release and then the parachute opened and I floated over farmland. I landed in a fruit tree and ended up caught by my harness and with my feet swinging a couple of feet above the ground.'

In 1990 Philipp Hess remembered that:
'In those moments of naked terror, I tried to release the obstacles, two oxygen bottles. Our legs were dangling out of the aircraft and the air stream was so strong that it pulled off my flying boots and my socks. Then suddenly I was free. I pulled the release, but the parachute only partly opened and I slammed barefoot on to the asphalt of a street (a tree might have been better!) As a result, I sustained an injury to a bone in my knee. I still suffer from it today.

'Besides a grazing shot on my arm and a shot in the shoulder, I had a broken lower jaw. Because of that, I later I lost all of my lower teeth. I escaped lightly but I am 30% disabled. My injuries might have been caused because we were too low when I baled out and so my parachute did not open properly. Or perhaps it had been damaged by gunfire during the combat and had too many holes in it.'

Both of Möllenbrok's companion aircraft were also lost in the attack, with fighters being responsible in each case. As mentioned earlier, one crashed at Whitstable, with the loss of the crew of four; the other was sufficiently damaged to cause it to crash near Calais, shortly after the crew had baled out. In spite of their injuries, it transpired that Heinz Möllenbrok and Philipp Hess were the lucky ones among their own crew. Their aircraft spread itself across two fields at Summerfield Farm, Staple, eastern Kent; the bodies of Reineke and Golob, both of whom were just short of 21-years old, were found in a cornfield near the village of Ash.

Sergeant Frederick William "Taffy" Higginson, pilot of the Hurricane that made the last attack on Heinz's Dornier, also did not make it back to base. His aircraft was hit by return gunfire and force-landed south of Whitstable at over 100mph. The aircraft was a 'write-off' but Higginson was only slightly injured and was flying again on 18 August.

Heinz landed in a fruit tree at Summerfield Farm. He was found by two farm workers (Ron Cryer and Arthur "Curly" Wanstall), who managed to release him and get him down—after initially threatening him with a shotgun. They then took him to the farmhouse, where he was given a tot of whiskey 'medicine' and where the farmer's wife, Mrs Doris Vickers, a nurse who had served during the First World War, was able dress his wounds. Heinz explained that:

'My right arm had been badly injured (almost severed) and was hanging from only a strip of flesh, the bone having been smashed by bullets when we were attacked. I also had a shell splinter in my lung. The two men carried me into the farmhouse and the farmer's wife told them to put me on the sofa —but I was losing a lot of blood and I did not want to spoil her furniture so I asked for a chair instead. She was very gentle and kind as she attended to me and I have never forgotten her kindness. I was badly injured but I was just so thankful to have survived and thankful for the help I received at the farm'.

Later that day, Heinz and Hess travelled together to Chartham Hospital, near Canterbury, where Heinz subsequently had cause to be grateful to Dr. Mair, a young surgeon of German origin. Mair was opposed to the immediate amputation of Heinz's injured arm and managed to sew it back together. Although the arm required two further operations at the Royal Herbert Hospital, Woolwich at a later date, Mair's skill saved it from amputation, though it never again functioned properly.

After Chartham, Möllenbrok and Hess were both transferred to the Royal Herbert Hospital, Woolwich, where Heinz was to stay for seven months and, together with his fellow Luftwaffe patients, was cared for by nursing staff throughout the night bombing Blitz of 1940-41. Hess did not stay quite as long: after four weeks at the Royal Herbert Hospital, he was transferred to a PoW camp in Oldham. In January 1941, he sailed from Glasgow to Canada in the *Duchess of York*. With him on the voyage was Oberleutnant Franz von Werra, who later achieved fame as *The One that Got Away* when he escaped from a Canadian PoW camp, made his way to the United States and eventually got back to Germany. After the war, Hess was an engineer at the Opel plant in Rüsselheim and eventually retired to Waldbronn. He died there in 1995.

After seven months' recuperation at Woolwich, Heinz was transferred to a PoW camp at Donaldson's School, Edinburgh. He was later transferred to the Shap Wells Hotel, Shap, (Camp 15) on edge of Lake District, which had been converted into a PoW camp to accommodate more than 200 officers, mainly from U-boats. The state of his injuries qualified him for a prisoner exchange scheme and Heinz had hopes of being back in Germany for Christmas 1941. However, a projected exchange of badly-wounded prisoners via Newhaven collapsed in October 1941 and he was posted instead to prison camps at Godalming (Camp 23) and then Swanwick (Camp 13), Derbyshire. The latter, which is now the Hayes Conference Centre, was the camp from which Franz von Werra (*The One That Got Away*) had escaped in one of his earlier attempts to get home. After eighteen months at Swanwick, Heinz was sent to Chepstow for another operation.

In October 1943, he was taken to Glasgow, where 350 badly-wounded Germans awaited repatriation. Other prisoners of war came from Canada and from the USA until there were some 1,000 in total. They were subsequently taken by ship to Gothenburg, Sweden, where the exchange was made against the same number of badly-wounded British servicemen, and were then repatriated to Germany. It is believed that it was the first such exchange to take place; there were others through Algiers, Barcelona and Switzerland between 1943 and 1945. Prior to repatriation, Heinz was promoted to Oberleutnant and in January 1944 he was awarded the Iron Cross Second Class and the Wound Badge in Silver. He had two more operations on his return to Germany. After the war, he became a farmer and settled in Schleswig-Holstein.

Möllenbrok re-visited England for the first time in 1990 (to participate in the Thames TV Programme *The Blitz*) and met Sheila Bambridge, the nurse who had looked after him at Woolwich. He also revisited some of his old PoW camps in the south of England and laid wreaths on the graves of his old comrades. During his visit he explained that :
'Both Hess and I could not totally dismiss the loss of our two comrades.
We still remain shocked by it. I had always wanted to visit their graves

in England, but I was able to do it only this year—and with English help. I did it so that I could send pictures of their graves to their relatives, who have been immediately grateful, even in cases where the mother had already died.'

He returned to England a number of times after that, usually to re-trace old steps and to locate and identify those Luftwaffe fliers who were not identified at the time of their burial and whose headstone simply states: *Ein Deutscher Soldat.* In 1998 he told me that:

'I think it is my duty to find as many (of his old comrades) *as I can. Not just from KG2 but also from other Luftwaffe units. Tracing the dead, finding out what happened to them and letting mothers, widows and relatives know is very important. It helps them and it ensures that such things will never happen again.'*

In May 1998, he renewed his acquaintance with the Vickers family in Kent, and shook the hand of Denis, who as a five-year-old had seen Heinz parachute on to his grandparents' farm and had watched his grandmother bathing and dressing Heinz's wounds before soldiers arrived to take the German away. He also met 'Bob' Cryer, the farm-worker who had taken him prisoner in August 1940. He even tracked down 'Taffy' Higginson, the Hurricane pilot with whom he had shared a dangerous episode fifty-eight years earlier. In October 1998, Heinz returned to England again—as the KG2 representative at the funeral of Heinrich Richter . On that occasion, he stayed with my wife and I for five days, during which we took the opportunity to visit the Shap Wells Hotel, long since returned to its pre-war purpose, and German airmen's graves in cemeteries at Hylton (Sunderland) and at Thornaby, where the graves of his own countrymen lie side by side with those of Allied airmen.

Heinz expressed his feelings

Heinz Möllenbrok stepping ashore at Gothenburg, Sweden, October 1943.
[Imperial War Museum]

regarding the graves he had visited, and the waste that war brings, when he was interviewed at my home by David Lorimer for an article that appeared in the *Evening Gazette* on 14 October 1998, the day of Richter's funeral. The following is an extract

' *"They did their best for their country,"* he said. Then he reflects on the RAF's toll of WWII dead and missing. *"They all did, they all did." For though today's wreath is for Heinrich Richter, who like Heinz also flew with KG2, its "dedication" also remembers Allied airmen. He has no anger against his former enemies, only respect. That goes for the Hurricane pilot who brought his war to an abrupt end over Kent.*

"When I go to the Royal Air Force Memorial at Runnymede, I see a memorial to the 20,000 men who went missing in action and have no known grave. We remember them too on our wreaths. It is about remembrance; remembrance together. And I remember what it says on that memorial at Runnymede: "Their Name Liveth for Evermore."

"When I reflect on those who died in London, in Berlin, the firestorms of Hamburg and in the catastrophe of Dresden, where who knows how many died, I think that it should never happen again. The faults of the politicians were paid for by the people, the people of all countries."

My friend Heinz Möllenbrok died at his home in Preetz, Schleswig-Holstein, on 16 December 2007.

Heinz Möllenbrok in 1998.
[Trevor Smith]

Broken Eagles:
Luftwaffe crashes in Cleveland, 1939-1943

The RAF section at Acklam Road cemetery, Thornaby, includes the graves of both RAF and Luftwaffe personnel [Author]

The 're-discovery' of the Dornier bomber at South Bank in November 1997 proved to be a novel and exciting experience for the local population, but crashes of Luftwaffe aircraft in the Teesside area were not uncommon during the Second World War. At least seventy-two German aircraft crashed in Yorkshire or off its coastline during the 1939-1945 conflict and at least fourteen of those came down in Cleveland or in the surrounding countryside. Three of them came to earth within eight miles of Middlesbrough and two crashed in the sea off the Cleveland coast, but few came to grief while making a deliberate attempt to bomb targets in the area.

Several of the crashes put Teesside into the record books of the Second World War. On 17 October 1939, three Catterick-based Spitfires of No.41 Squadron shot down a Heinkel 111 (F6+PK) of *2./Aufklärungsruppe122* some twenty miles east of Whitby while it was on reconnaissance sortie to the Firth

1939. Bernhard Hochstuhl (2nd from left) and Eugen Lange (right), survivors of the 'Sandsend' Heinkel 111, arrive in London. [Author's collection]

of Forth to locate the battle-cruiser HMS *Hood*. The two crewmen who survived were adrift in a dinghy for two days before they were washed ashore north of Sandsend and became the first German fliers to be captured on English soil during the Second World War. Four months later, a Heinkel 111 (wnr..2323; 1H+FM) of *4./Kampfgeschwader26* on anti-shipping patrol became the first enemy aircraft to crash on English soil when it belly-landed at Bannial Flatt Farm, Whitby, on 3 February 1940. It was shot down by three Hurricanes from No.43 Squadron, Acklington, led by Peter Townsend, who later became romantically involved with Princess Margaret. And on 3 April 1940, fighters scored a less-acceptable 'first' when a No.41 Squadron Spitfire and a Heinkel 111 (1H+AC of *Stab II/Kampfgeschwader 26*) on anti-shipping patrol shot each other down some fifteen miles off Whitby.

The Spitfire (serial.N3114) went into the record books as the first fighter to be lost in the defence of this country during World War Two. The crews of both planes were rescued by trawlers, the Luftwaffe crew being picked up by the Scarborough trawler *Silver Line*, which had machine-gunned the bomber

3 February 1940. He.111 of 4./KG26 at Bannial Flatt Farm. [Courtesy of The Northern Echo]

3 April 1940. A Spitfire of No.41 Squadron, Catterick, and a Heinkel 111 of Stab II/KG26 shot down each other some fifteen miles off Whitby. An artist's impression by John Moore. [Author]

just before it ditched.

These early interceptions occurred over the sea, at a time when attacks on shipping were paramount, but from the summer of 1940 confrontations increasingly took place over land. No.41 Squadron scored again on 11 August 1940, when three of its Spitfires caught a Junkers 88 of *1./ Aufklärungsgruppe121* (wnr.2086; 7A+KH) over Helmsley as it was returning from a reconnaissance flight over aerodromes at Dishforth and Linton-on-Ouse. The Junkers belly-landed alongside the Sandsend road on Newton Moor, near Scaling Dam. The Spitfires had further success days later when they downed a Messerschmitt 110 long-range fighter of *Zerstörergeschwader 76* (M8+CH) over Barnard Castle during the large daylight raid on North East England on 15 August 1940.

The Messerschmitt was one of a number of enemy aircraft claimed by northern-based fighter squadrons on that day - the day the Luftwaffe came to know as *'Black Thursday'*.

These successes were won by fighters, but bad weather took its toll in almost equal measure. On 1 November 1940, a low-flying Junkers 88 of *8./ Kampfgeschwader 30*

November 1940. The wreck of Ju.88 4D+TS on Glaisdale Head. [Author's Collection]

March 1941. *Personnel from No.41 Squadron, Catterick, inspect the wreckage of Ju.88 4U+GH on Eston Hills.* [Courtesy of The Northern Echo]

(4D+TS; wnr..7089) on a bombing mission to Linton-on-Ouse fell foul of bad weather and struck the hillside at Glaisdale Head, west of Whitby, although there is a suggestion that anti-aircraft fire might also have played a part. On 30 March 1941, No.41 Squadron Spitfires shot down a Junkers 88 (4U+GH wnr..0115) of *1./Aufklärungsgruppe 123* that was on armed reconnaissance to Manchester and caused it to dive vertically into the peat on Eston Hills, near Middlesbrough. But on 4 June 1941 it was bad weather which resulted in a Junkers 88 night fighter of *2./Nachtjagdgeschwader 2* (RA+LK; wnr..0570;) piling in at Skelder Moor, just north of Whitby, and on 10 July it was poor visibility which caused a low-flying Junkers 88 of *2./Küstenfliegergruppe 106* (M2+EK; wnr..2227) to clip the high cliffs at Staithes and disintegrate across the high shoulder of upland known as Quarry Bank

Collision with a balloon cable was the immediate cause of the demise of the low-flying Dornier 217E-4 of *8./Kampfgeschwader 2* (U5+HS; wnr..5314) that crashed at South Bank on the 15 January 1942, but anti-aircraft fire from the steamer *Empire Bay,* anchored off the Tees, caused the initial damage. The steamer was badly damaged by the Dornier and sank in Tees Bay that evening.

Typhoon fighters from RAF Acklington (Northumberland) took the credit for the daytime interception of two Messerschmitt 210 fighter-bombers of *Kampfgeschwader 6* off the Tees on 6 September 1942—and for their subsequent destruction. One (2H+CA; wnr..2348) came down alongside the Redcar reservoir at New Marske; the other(wnr..2321; 2H+HA) crashed at Sledgates, Robin Hood's Bay. The Messerchmitts were the first 210s to be shot down over Britain.

It is believed that a combination of anti-aircraft fire and bad weather caused

December, 1942. *The burial of the crew of the 'Wheeldale Moor' Dornier at Acklam Road cemetery, Thornaby.* [via Steve Hall]

the demise of two Dornier 217s on route to bomb York on 17 December 1942. One of them, of *7./Kampfgeschwader 2* (U5+GR;wnr..4342) crashed at Crow Nest, near the Bilsdale village of Hawnby; the other, belonging to *2./ Kampfgeschwader 2* (U5+AK; wnr..5600), disintegrated when it caught the high ground of Wheeldale Moor, near Goathland, west of Whitby. The last German aircraft to crash on land in the Teesside area was also a Dornier 217 (wnr..5441; U5+BL*).* It belonged to *3./Kampfgeschwader 2* and it crashed at Great Stainton (Co. Durham) after being shot down over Darlington by a Scorton-based Beaufighter of No.219 Squadron on the night of 11/12 March 1943.

Thirty-four *Luftwaffe* crews were lost in the above operations and most of them were buried in the RAF plot at Acklam Road cemetery, Thornaby-on-Tees, where they still lie. Of the thirteen RAF pilots who were involved in those incidents, only six survived the war.

Over the years, one-time foes have extended the hand of friendship towards each other. Peter Townsend, whose bullets almost severed the leg of Heinkel gunner Karl Missy on 3 February 1940, established contact with Missy after the war and remained in touch with his former foe until Missy died in 1981. In October 1979, 'Sandsend' survivors, Eugen Lange and Bernhard Hochstuhl, returned to Cleveland to thank those involved in their rescue forty years earlier. In December 1999, I put Lange and Hochstuhl in touch with their former adversary, Spitfire pilot Ted Shipman, and the three exchanged Christmas wishes until the Germans died in the mid-1990s. Shipman died in August 1998, but prior to that he was also in regular contact with the Messerschmitt 110 pilot whom he had first met in a dangerous encounter over County Durham on 15 August 1940. And in 1990 Rudolf Behnisch, the pilot of the Heinkel 111 shot down off Whitby on 3 April 1940, kept a promise he made to himself fifty years earlier: he returned to Scarborough to thank those who had saved his life. Bob Watkinson, who had plucked Behnisch from the sea in 1940, had died some years before but his son took his place at an emotional meeting in Bridlington on the anniversary of the rescue.

Luftwaffe War Graves
in Acklam Road cemetery, Thornaby

At the cessation of hostilities in 1945, some 6,000 German dead of two world wars lay buried in municipal cemeteries and village churchyards in more than 700 different locations around Britain. The toll included those who had died in captivity, crew members from World War I airships, dead who had been washed ashore and crews of crashed war planes.

In the late 1950s, steps were taken to establish a German military cemetery on Cannock Chase, Staffordshire, to which all German war dead buried in Great Britain and Northern Ireland might ultimately be transferred. On 16 October 1959, an agreement signed by the governments of Britain and the Federal Republic of Germany empowered the German equivalent of the Commonwealth War Graves Commission, the *Volksbund Deutsche Kriegsgräberfürsorge e.V.*, to take responsibility for the creation of the cemetery and the transfer of German war dead to it.

The first programme of re-burials occurred during 1962-1963 and that was followed by a second during 1966-1967. The consecration of the Cannock German War Cemetery (*Deutschen Soldatenfriedhof*) took place on 10 July 1967, when it was opened to the public. 4,939 German dead lie there: 2,143 from World War I and 2,796 from World War II.

However, not all German war dead in Britain have been transferred to Cannock Chase. In some instances, relatives refused to grant permission for exhumation; in other cases, graves could not be opened because Germans had been interred with Britain civilians in communal plots. In addition, where Germans had been buried in British local war cemeteries, local authorities were reluctant to agree to removals if the effect would be to destroy the overall appearance of the burial plots.

Thus, although most German war dead in Britain have now been transferred to Cannock, 263 from the 1914-1918 war and 1,044 from the 1939-1945 conflict still rest in the churchyards and cemeteries to which they were originally allocated. It is believed that 954 of this number are Luftwaffe personnel who lost their lives in operations against this country during the Second World War.

There are five sites in North East England that have become the final resting places for seventy-nine Luftwaffe aircrew who failed to return home. Four of those sites are at Broomhill (near Amble, Northumberland), Hylton (near Sunderland), Brandesburton (near Hornsea, East Yorkshire) and Hull. The fifth site is Acklam Road cemetery, Thornaby, where twenty-nine Luftwaffe aircrew are buried. The following lists gives their names and a brief account of the circumstances leading to their demise.

Acklam Road Cemetery,
Thornaby.

Date	Rank	Name	Aircraft	Unit	Code
1940					
1 Nov.	Feldwebel	Wilhelm Wowereit	Junkers 88	8./KG30	4D+TS
	Oberfeldwebel	Hans Schulte-Mater			(wnr.. 7089)
	Unteroffizier	Alfred Rodermond			
	Unteroffizier	Gerhard Pohling			

Struck the hillside at Glaisdale Head near Whitby, at c.5.00pm, while en route to attack the aerodrome at Linton-on-Ouse. Precise cause is currently unknown, though poor visibility is suspected (eye-witnesses claim that it was foggy). However, there is also the suggestion that anti-aircraft fire might have played a part.

Date	Rank	Name	Aircraft	Unit	Code
1941					
30 March	Unteroffizier	Hans Steigerwald	Junkers 88	1(F)./123	4U+GH
					(wnr. 0115)

Was on an armed reconnaissance sortie to Manchester when it was intercepted over south Durham by two Spitfires of No.41 Squadron, Catterick. It was shot down by ex-Ampleforth schoolboy Flight Lieutenant Tony Lovell and crashed on Eston Hills, Teesside, at 3.15pm, exploding on impact. Steigerwald baled out but his parachute failed to open properly and he fell to his death among the trees that line Flatts Lane, Normanby. Other crew members—Leutnant Wolfgang Schlott, Leutnant Otto Meingold and Feldwebel Wilhelm Schmigale—were never found.

Date	Rank	Name	Aircraft	Unit	Code
27 April	Oberleutnant	Hildebrand	Junkers 88	KüFlGr.	M2+JL
		Voigtländer-Tetzner		3./106	(wnr. 2234)

Crashed into the sea off Amble, Northumberland, on 13 March. Was on a sortie to Glasgow went it was shot down by Flight Lieutenant Desmond Sheen, in a Spitfire of No.72 Squadron, Acklington, Northumberland. Voigtländer-Tetzner's body was recovered from the sea, one mile South-east of the Heugh Light, Hartlepool, on 27 April 1941. He was buried under that date because the actual date of his death was unknown at the time. Other crew members—Leutnant Rudolf Dietze, Obergefreiter Walter Wesserer and Obergefreiter Hans Vandamme—missing, believed killed.

4 June	Leutnant	Johannes Feuerbaum	Junkers 88	NJG 2	R4+LK
	Gefreiter	Gerhard Denzin			(wnr..0570)
	Gefreiter	Rudolf Peters			

Was on a night intruder sortie and had just crossed in near Whitby when it crashed on Skelder Moor in conditions of poor visibility.

10 July	Oberleutnant	Edgar Peisart	Junkers 88	KüFlGr	M2+EK
	Leutnant	Rudolf Bellof		2./106	(wnr. 2227)
	Gefreiter	Gerhard Vogel			
	Feldwebel	Karl Kinder			

One of three aircraft briefed to carry out anti-shipping operations between Holy Island and Whitby. Peisart reached his patrol line but encountered mist and flew into cliffs below Cliff Farm, Staithes, at 00.06am. The two other aircraft suffered at similar fate: they crashed at Speeton, near Filey.

10 Nov.	Oberfähnrich	Karl Schütz	Junkers 88	KüFlGr.	S4+HK
	Oberfeldwebel	Werner Hanel		2./506	(wnr. 1409)
	Oberleutnant	Heinz Weber*			

Shot down by HMS *Quantock* while attacking a convoy off Ravenscar, near Robin Hoods Bay. Crashed on the shore line below the steep cliffs of Blea Wyke Point at c. 5.30pm. The fourth crew member, Unteroffizier Arthur Gräber, was not found and was listed as 'missing'. *Heinz Weber is currently buried in the grave marked *Ein Deutscher Soldat* (A German Soldier) because his identity had not been established when he was buried. His identity has now been established beyond doubt. The German authorities are now aware of this and steps are being taken to change the headstone.

1942

15 Jan.	Feldwebel	Joachim Lehnis	Dornier 217	8./KG2	U5+HS
	Leutnant	Rudolf Matern			(wnr. 5314)
	Unteroffizier	Hans Maneke			
	Oberfeldwebel	Heinrich Richter			

Was on an anti-shipping sortie when it attacked the ss *Empire Bay*, which was at anchor off Hartlepool. Was damaged by anti-aircraft fire from the vessel before it collided with a barrage balloon cable near Smith's Tees Dock and crashed on to railway sidings at South Bank, Middlesbrough. Crashed at 6.10pm. Although none of the estimated five bombs aimed at the ship actually found their target, they exploded close enough to irreparably damage the *Empire Bay*. It sank in Tees Bay hours later after the crew had been taken off by the pilot cutter *W.R. Lister*, captained by Tees pilot Bill Young.

| 31 Aug. | Oberfeldwebel | Paul Kolodzie | Junkers 88 | 3./KG77 | 3Z+CB |
| | Gefreiter | Josef Sanden | | | wnr. 0144146) |

Shot down off Sunderland on 28 August. The victor was originally thought to have been Flight Lieutenant J.R.B Firth (with Pilot Officer R.G. Harding) of No. 406 Squadron, Scorton. However, it now seems likely that the credit should go to Flight Lieutenant Horne (with Sergeant Alcock) in a Beaufighter of No. 219 Squadron, Acklington. Two other members of the German crew—Oberfeldwebel Alfred Reidel and Feldwebel Josef Pfeffer—baled out and were captured.

| **6 Sept.** | Feldwebel | Heinrich Mösges | Me. 210 | 16./KG6 | 2H+CA |
| | Obergefreiter | Eduard Czerny | | | (wnr.. 173) |

One of a pair believed to have been on armed reconnaissance when intercepted over the Tees by two Typhoons of No.1 Squadron, Acklington, Northumberland. This aircraft was shot down by Pilot Officer Perrin and crashed at Fell Briggs Farm, New Marske at c. 1145am. The crew baled out but neither parachute opened. The second Me.210 was pursued as far as Robin Hoods Bay before it was shot down by Perrin's No.2, Pilot Officer Bridges. The crew baled out and were captured.

17 Dec.	Feldwebel	Wilhelm Stoll	Dornier 217	2./KG2	U5+AK
	Obergefreiter	Hans Roeschner			(wnr. 5600)
	Obergefreiter	Gerhard Wicht			
	Obergefreiter	Franz Armann			

This aircraft crashed at Ravenstones, Wheeldale Moor, near Goathland, while on route to attack York. It is thought that it was hit by anti-aircraft fire some fifteen miles east of the crash site. It then went through some bad weather before striking the moor. The same evening, a second Do.217 (of 7./KG2) crashed into the hillside at Crow Nest, near Hawnby, some six miles north-west of Helmsley.

1943

| **30 June** | Unteroffizier | Karl Roos | Dornier 217 | 6./KG2 | U5+DP |
| | | | | | (wnr.. 4584) |

Shot down in the early hours of 16 May 1943 thirty-five miles east of Sunderland by Flying Officer B.R. Keele (with Flying Officer G. Cowles), flying a Beaufighter of No. 604 Squadron, Scorton, near Richmond. Roos' body was washed ashore at Blackhall Rocks on 30 June and he was buried under that date. The body of crew member Unteroffizier Bruno Mittelstadt was also washed ashore and was later buried at Castletown cemetery near Sunderland. Other crew members—Obergefreiter Günter Kaeber and Unteroffizier Alfred Richter—were never found.

**German Air Force terms
used in the text: Luftwaffe ranks**
(with roughly equivalent RAF ranks)

Gefreiter (Gefr.)	Aircraftman 1st Class (AC1)
Unteroffizier (Uffz.)	Corporal (Cpl)
Feldwebel (Fw.)	Sergeant (Sgt)
Oberfeldwebel (Obfw.)	Flight Sergeant (F/Sgt)
Oberfähnrich zur See (Ofhr.)	Senior Midshipman (naval rank)
Leutnant (Lt.)	Pilot Officer (P/O)
Oberleutnant (Oblt.)	Flying Officer (F/O)

Luftwaffe losses in the Yorkshire area, 1939-1945
(by cause and location)

Date	Aircraft	Unit	Code	wnr.	Cause	Location
17.10.39	He.11H-1	2.(F)/122	F6+PK	?	Spitfire	off Whitby
21.10.39	He.115B	KüFlGr. 1./406	S4+EH	?	Hurricane	off Spurn Head
10.11.39	Do..18D	KüFlGr. 3./406	K6+DL	?	Hudson	off Scarborough
3.02.40	He.111H-3	4./KG26	1H+FM	2323	Hurricane	Whitby
3.04.40	He.111H-3	StabII./KG26	1H+AC	?	Spitfire	off Redcar
25/26.6.40	He.11P-2	3./KG4	5J+BL	?	Spitfire	Humber
1.07.40	He.111H-4	3./KG4	5J+EL	?	Spitfire	off Humber
1.07.40	He.115	KüFlGr.3./106	M2+CL	?	Tech.prob.	off Whitby
8.07.40	Ju.88A-1	9./KG4	5J+AT	3094	Fighter	Aldbrough, nr Hull
9.08.40	He.111H-4	2./KG4	5J+?K	?	Flak?	off NE coast?
11.08.40	Ju.88-1	1(F)/121	7A+KH	2086	Spitfire	Scaling,nr Whitby
15.08.40	Ju.88	7./KG30	4D+DR	?	Spitfire	Bridlington
15.08.40	Ju.88A-5	3./KG30	4D+KL	?	Hurricane	nr Bridlington
15.08.40	Ju.88	4./KG30	4D+?M	?	Hurricane	nr Bridlington
15.08.40	Ju.88	7./KG30	4D+?R	?	Fighter?	off Bridlington?
20.08.40	Ju.88A-1	8./KG30	4D+IS	?	Hurricane	Ottringham
21.08.40	He.111H-2	9./KG53	A1+?T	?	Spitfire	off Scarborough
27.10.40	Ju.88A-5	7./KG4	5J+ER	6129	Flak	Duggleby, nr Malton
27.10.40	Ju.88A-1	8./KG4	5J+HS	6048	Flak	off Tees?
1.11.40	Ju.88A-1	8./KG30	4D+TS	7089	eather?	Glaisdale Head
9.02.41	Ju.88A-5	4./KG30	4D+FM	8102	Fighter?	off Humber?
30.03.41	Ju.88A	1(F)/123	4U+GH	0115	Spitfire	Eston Hills, Teesside
8.04.41	Ju.88A-5	2./KG30	4D+UK	0541	Tech. Prob	off Humber?
15/16.04.41	He.111H-5	3./KG53	A1+AL	0370	Tech. prob?	Huby, nr York
4/5.05.41	Ju.88A-5	6./KG77	3Z+FP	7117	Tech prob?	off Bridlington
4/5.05.41	Ju.88A-5	KüFlGr.2./106	M2+DK	0656	Nightfighter	off Humber?
8.05.41	He.111H-5	Stab1./KG4	5J+ZB	3987	Hurricane	Withernssea
8/9.05.41	He.111P-4	6./KG55	G1+FP	3000	Defiant NF	nr Beverley
8/9.05.41	He.111H-5	4./KG53	A1+FM	4006	Defiant NF	nr Spurn Point

Date	Type	Unit	Code	Cause	Serial	Location
8/9.05.41	He.111H-5	6./KG53	A1+CW	Defiant NF	4042	Patrington, nr Hull
15.05.41	Ju.88A-5	6./KG1	VA+GP	Naval flak	6263	off Spurn Head
2/3.06.41	Ju.88C-4	2./NJG2	R4+LK	Weather	0570	nr Whitby
9/10.07.41	Ju.88A-5	KüFlGr.3./106	M2+AL	Weather?	4386	nr Filey
9/10.07.41	Ju.88A-5	KüFlGr 3./106	M2+CL	Weather?	3245	nr Filey
9/10.07.41	Ju.88A-5	KüFlGr 2./106	M2+EK	Weather?	2227	Staithes
11.07.41	He.111H-4	8./KG4	5J+ES	unknown	3956	off Humber
2.08.41	Ju.88	KuFlGr 1./506	S4+LH	Spitfire?	723	off Flamborough?
8.08.41	Bf.110C-5	1(F)/123	4U+XH	Spitfire	2306	off Flamborough?
10.11.41	Ju.88A-4	KuFlGr 2./506	S4+HK	Naval flak	1409	Ravenscar
15.01.42	Do.217E-4	8./KG2	U5+HS	Naval flak	5314	South Bank, Teesside
19.01.42	Ju.88A-5	3(F)/122	F6+PL	Spitfire	440	off Whitby
18.02.42	Do.217E-4	7./KG2	U5+KR	Spitfire	5342	off Humber
26/27.02.42	Do.217E-4	9./KG2	U5+ST	Unknown	1176	Humber area?
27/28.02.42	Do.217E	8./KG2	U5+AS	Naval flak	5346	Humber area?
8/9.03.42	Do.217E-4	9./KG2	U5+LT	Unknown	5336	Humber area?
28/29. 04.42	Do.217E-2	6./KG2	U5+KP	Nightfighter	1164	Coneysthorpe
28/29.04.42	Ju.88A-5	11/KG77	3Z+AV	Beaufighter	0289	off Whitby
28/29.04.42	Ju.88D-1	KüFlGr.1./106	M2+CH	Nightfighter	1334	Elvington
7/8.07.42	Do.217E-4	4./KG2	U5+BM	Nightfighter	5465	off Scarborough or Tyne
21.07.42	Do.217E-4	1./KG2	U5+IH	Mosquito	4260	off Spurn Head?
28/29.08.42	Do.217E-4	1./KG2	U5+FH	Beaufighter	5341	off Whitby?
6.09.42	Me.210A-1	16./KG6	2H+CA	Typhoon	2348	New Marske
6.09.42	Me.210A-1	16./KG6	2H+HA	Typhoon	2331	nr Robin Hoods Bay
23/24.09.42	Do.217E-4	1./KG2	U5+FH	Beaufighter	4294	off Flamborough
17.12.42	Do.217E-4	2./KG2	U5+AK	Flak	4348	nr Goathland
17.12.42	Do.217E-4	7./KG2	U5+GR	Low flying?	4342	Hawnby, nr Helmsley
3.01.43	Do.217E-4	9./KG2	U5+KT	Flak	4314	Skeffling
15/16.01.43	Do.217E-4	9./KG2	U5+AT	Mosquito?	4272	Humber area?
3.02.43	Do.217E-4	3./KG2	U5+GL	Beaufighter	5462	Muston, nr Filey
11.03.43	Do.217E-4	6./KG40	F8+LP	Beaufighter	5313	off Yorks coast.
15/16 .03.43	Ju.88A-14	2./KG6	3E+WK	Beaufighter	4532	off Spurn Head?
13/14. 06.43	Do.217E-4	5./KG2	U5+BN	Beaufighter?	4376	off Flamborough?

Date	Aircraft	Unit	Code	Werke No.	Cause	Location
12/13.07.43	Do.217K-1	4./KG2	U5+EM	4478	Mosquito?	off Humber?
13/14.07.43	Do.217M-1	3./KG2	U5+EL	56153	Beaufighter?	off Scarborough?
24/25.07.43	Do.217M-1	2./KG2	U5+HK	6058	Unknown	off Humber?
24/25.07.43	Do.217E-4	5./KG2	U5+DN	5489	Flak?	off Humber
25/26.07.43	Do.217M-1	2./KG2	U5+GK	6045	Beaufighter	off Spurn Head
25/26.07.43	Do.217K-1	Stab./KG2	U5+BA	4412	Beaufighter	off Spurn Head
25/26.07.43	Do.217E-4	5./KG2	U5+AN	4395	Flak	Long Riston
21/22.09.43	Do.217K-1	4./KG2	U5+CM	4620	Low flying	nr Withernsea
2/3.10.43	Ju.88E-1	2./KG66	Z6+GK	260175	Low flying?	off Spurn Head
04.03.45	Ju.88G-6	13./NJG3	D5+AX	620028	Low flying	Elvington, nr York

Bibliography

National Archives, Kew.
Report of an interview with Capt E.S Parks of the ss Empire Bay. ADM199/2139

Teesside Archives
Air raid files. Raid No.21. CB/M/C/40/12

Other archives
Air Intelligence Crashed Enemy Aircraft. Report No.118, 16 January 1942
     (Author's collection)

Books
Anon: *Roof over Britain: the official story of the AA defences, 1939-42.* HMSO
Balke, Ulf: *Der Luftkrieg in Europa; die Operativen Einsätze des Kampfgeschwaders 2
     im Zweiten Weltkrieg* Bernard & Graefe Verlag, Koblenz 1990
Norman, Bill: *Luftwaffe over the North* Pen & Sword Books Ltd (1993; 1997)
Norman, Bill: *Broken Eagles: Luftwaffe Losses over Yorkshire, 1939-1945.* Pen &
     Sword Books Ltd 2001
Ramsay, Winston G (ed): *The Blitz then & now.* vol.1 Battle of Prints International Ltd,
     1987
Ramsay, Winston G (ed): *The Blitz then & now.* vol.3 Battle of Prints International Ltd,
     1990
Shaw, David and Winfield, Barry: *Dive North East.* Underwater World Press. 1988
Smith, J.R & Kay, A.L: *German Aircraft of the Second World War.* Putnam 1972

Journals & Newspapers
Evening Gazette, Middlesbrough. 16 Jan. 1942; 19 Jan.1942; 8 Dec. 1945; 27 Nov.
     1997; 14 Oct. 1998; 17 Nov. 1998; 29 Dec. 1998; 15 Jan. 2002
Mail on Sunday, London. 11 Oct. 1998
Northern Daily Mail, Hartlepool. 16 Jan. 1942; 19 Jan. 1942; 12 Mar. 1943; 19 Apr.
     1945;
RAF News. 12 Dec. 1997
Smith, Leonard G: *Eagle Attack: Luftkrieg gegen England.* In Newsletter of the
     Shoreham Local History Society   Date unknown but c. 2004

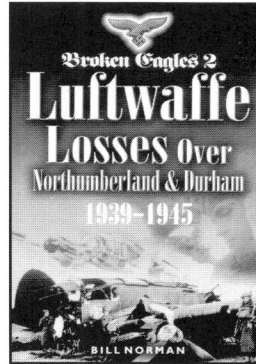

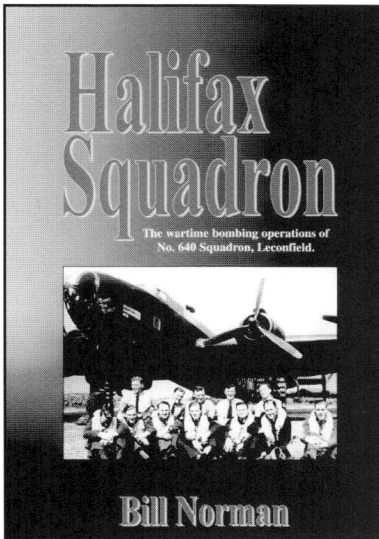

Some press comments about Bill Norman's books

Luftwaffe over the North (1993; 1997).
'This is one of those excellent books which takes a look at a small portion of the Second World War and makes the parts played by ordinary people come alive.'
[*Yorkshire Gazette & Herald, York*]
'A moving record of the waste as well as the heroism of war.'
 [*Northern Echo, Darlington*]

Failed to Return (1995)
'A moving testament to the courage of ordinary people who did extraordinary things.'
[*Evening Gazette, Middlesbrough*]
'A treasure-trove for students of the air war and a fitting tribute to those who volunteered to take the war to the night skies of Germany.'
[*Telegraph & Argus, Bradford*]

No.640(Halifax)Squadron (1999).
'An excellent history of 640 Squadron...a meticulously researched book with many appendices. All Halifax and 4 Group 'buffs' need a copy.'
[*Intercom, Journal of the Aircrew Association*]

Broken Eagles (2001).
'A thorough and interesting record of dramatic events, told from both sides of the conflict'. [*Whitby Gazette, Whitby*]
'Using testaments from local eye-witnesses and British and German servicemen, *Broken Eagles* graphically recounts how Luftwaffe aircraft met their doom over the North East...' [*Evening Gazette, Middlesbrough*]
'The reports by German crews and British personnel make the book an exciting read and will stir the memories of those who took part…Appendices give details of all aircraft lost as well as listing crew losses in alphabetic order and by date…Although the book deals with only a small sector of the Front, it gives a very good insight into operations over England.' [*Luftwaffen-Revue* (Germany)]

Broken Eagles 2 (2002).
'As fascinating and as detailed as the last book...with everything we have come to expect from the series. Thoroughly recommended reading.'
[*The Circuit* (East Cleveland)]
'Bill Norman's descriptions of action make it exciting enough for the general reader, while the technical detail should satisfy aviation enthusiasts...His meticulous research has been helped by former German airmen..' [*The Echo, Sunderland*]

Wartime Teesside revisited (2004).
'An excellent read and is a must for all who are interested in local history.'
[*Now & Then magazine* (Teesside)]

__Halifax Squadron__ (2005)
'A great addition to the 'library' of the RAF's wartime bomber offensive'.
 [*FlyPast* **Magazine**]
'A well-researched and well-written book that will please many historians'
 [*Aviation World*]
'Having reviewed many squadron histories over the years, I can confidently say that
this is one of the very best'. [**A/Cdre Graham Pitchfork,** *Aircrew Association*]
'Any surviving veteran is sure to say: "Yes, this is what it was like." Readers of a
later generation will be moved—and humbled—by the unhesitating heroism. This is a
magnificent record.' [*Northern Echo* , **Darlington**]

Northern Echo

Middlesbrough-born writer Bill Norman is an aviation historian with a particular interest in the North-East of England. For many years he has been researching the air war over the northern counties of Yorkshire, Durham and Northumberland during the Second World War and he has written numerous articles on that theme for the northern press and for a number of aviation magazines. He has also written eight books on the subject, most of which were published by Leo Cooper/Pen & Sword. More recently, Bill has started publishing under his own imprint. This is his third such effort and follows his very successful publications *Wartime Teesside revisited (*2004) and *Halifax Squadron* (2005).

Photographer Stuart McMillan (Tel. 01287—651491) was present at the funeral of Heinrich Richter and has a wide range of pictures for sale.